CAMPBELL
COLLEGE

CAMPBELL COLLEGE

KEITH HAINES

TEMPUS

Frontispiece: On 1 June 1951 Queen Elizabeth and Princess Margaret visited Campbell College to present the Charter of Incorporation (the amalgamation of the Trustees and Governors of the school).

Editorial note: *unless otherwise stated, where lists of names are included, they run left to right, and from back row to front row.*

First published 2004

Tempus Publishing Limited
The Mill, Brimscombe Port,
Stroud, Gloucestershire, GL5 2QG
www.tempus-publishing.com

© Keith Haines, 2004

The right of Keith Haines to be identified as the Author
of this work has been asserted in accordance with the
Copyrights, Designs and Patents Act 1988.

British Library Cataloguing in Publication Data.
A catalogue record for this book is available from the British Library.

ISBN 0 7524 3313 X

Typesetting and origination by Tempus Publishing Limited.
Printed in Great Britain.

Contents

Acknowledgements

Whatever faults Campbellians may have, it has to be acknowledged that many of them are undeniably generous. This volume could not have been compiled without the assistance of many former pupils – and others – who have shown considerable faith by donating personal, precious and unique images, and provided information.

The Headmaster of Campbell College, Dr Ivan Pollock, feels that there is a lack of justice in the principle of alphabetical order. In order to amuse him, therefore, I place this list of thanks (some of which are posthumous) in reverse order – with two exceptions:

Derry Whyte – and the Old Campbellian or OC Society (OC throughout this book stands for Old Campbellian) – who showed great interest in and commitment to the project; and Edward Beckett, nephew of Samuel Beckett, who deserves particular gratitude for proving immensely co-operative at very short notice.

Shaun Wilson, Kelly Wilson, Mrs Joyce Wilson, Mrs Tracy Williams (*née* Savage), Mrs Isabel Wightman, Mrs Betty Whiteside, Eric Waugh, Times Newspapers, St Mark's Parish Church, Michael Shanks, Brian Robinson, Performing Arts Department of the Arts Council of Northern Ireland, Christopher Pelly, Cecil Pedlow, Walter Paul, The Oxford Union, Prof Bill Morrison, Brendan Moran (*Sportsfile* image of Andrew Bree), Tony and Mrs Mary Moore, Mrs Anne Moody, Mrs Amy Mills, Revd John Miller, Mrs Annie Maxwell, Miranda MacQuitty, Mrs Betty MacQuitty, William J. McKee, Mark McKee, Mrs Doris McGuffin, Rona McAlpine, MAGNI, Mrs Lisa Lewis, John Knox, Prof James Knowlson, Beverley Kemp, Ken Kennedy, Walter Jones, ITN, Ian Irwin, Imperial War Museum, Holywood Parish Church, Dr Philip Hammond, Gordon Hamilton, John Hamilton, Gilbert & Soame photographers (Oxford Union photo), Dr John Green, Robin Gordon, Ada Gordon, Chris Gailey, David Fullerton, Andrew Fullerton, Patrick Freeman, F.M. Foley, Ian Feely, Mrs A.J. Emerson, Basil Devenish-Meares, Prof James Stevens Curl, Mrs Karen Crooks, Prof Harry Cronne, David Cronne, Mrs Moira Cresswell, Tom Corken, Rory Collins, Dr Tony Chase, Laurence Chase, Ronnie Caves, Michael and Mrs Naomi Caves, David Catherwood, Harry Cathcart, David and Mrs Barbara Calvert, Brian Byrne (photo of Philip Hammond), N.F.E. Burrows, Sqdn Ldr T.M. Bulloch, Mrs Ann Bree, Terence Bradley, Derrick Boyd, Jonathan Bleakley, Noel Ashfield, George Adams and Graham Acheson.

Convention demands that one's wife is thanked, but it is true to say that without Wilma's remarkable – even boundless – tolerance, this volume would never have seen the light of day.

Introduction
A Brief History of Campbell College

Now into its second century, there is an apparent confidence on the Belmont estate, as the registration approaches its largest total – 850 – and a substantial building project is completed. There would have been many amongst the original founders of Campbell College who would have regarded such developments as a vindication of their aspirations.

There is much of which Campbell College can be proud. Those educated on the Belmont demesne have visited every continent, and many of the remotest islands, of the globe. There is a proud record of public and military service, and of personal commercial and business success. There has been academic success with many Oxbridge entrants and around sixty university professorships, and a considerable range of sporting achievement, which includes over thirty Irish rugby internationals, including the most-capped Irish rugby player, Mike Gibson.

The school has also provided prominent figures in the media – journalists of international reputation, such as Arthur Moore and John Irvine; local news presenters such as Noel Thompson and Mike Nesbitt; and TV personalities such as Gordon Burns of *The Krypton Factor* and Charles Lawson of *Coronation Street*. There are unusual boasts – two mountain peaks (in Canada and Greenland) are named after former pupils, and two of the earliest alumni became personally acquainted with both modern Pahlavi Shahs of Iran.

One of the most overworked and inaccurate phrases used in relation to schools, however, is 'going from strength to strength' and, as in all institutions, there have been tensions, difficulties (financial and numerical), minor earthquakes and sub-texts which have belied the apparent placid progress towards consolidation. The reality is that, within three years of its foundation, Campbell College came perilously close to shutting its doors!

All schools accommodate – even if it proves a small exhibition – some sort of Rogues' Gallery. One of the staff at the Prep School (Cabin Hill) was to become one of the most celebrated secret agents of the Second World War, whilst a former pupil gained notoriety in 1940 for treason committed in the London Embassy of the United States, and was rewarded with six years' incarceration!

The school is pleased to claim a Regius Professor of Greek at Oxford University – E.R. Dodds – but his later admission was that his main ambition at school was to tar and feather the Headmaster, R.A.H. MacFarland, and indeed he was expelled for studied insolence towards the latter! A Nobel laureate – Samuel Beckett – taught briefly at Campbell in

1928. The Headmaster was incredulous that his employee should want to forego the pleasure of teaching 'the cream of Ulster'. Beckett remained proud of his immediate riposte: 'Yes, rich and thick'!

Foundation to the Second World War

Campbell College was established as the result of the bequest of Henry Campbell (*d.* 23 January 1889), who made his fortune from the local textile trade. Incorporating the best in contemporary academic philosophy, curriculum and structural features, the school was designed by noted Ulster architect, William Henry Lynn, and opened its doors to 215 pupils on 3 September 1894.

Differences of opinion between the joint-Headmasters resulted in one of them – Henry Parker – leaving within a year, and this served to create tensions between the survivor, James Adams McNeill, and his staff. The enforced departure of half of the latter resulted in 1897 in a legal *cause célèbre* in Dublin, which brought notoriety – and a reduced enrolment – from which the school only narrowly recovered. However, under McNeill the school attained considerable academic success with Oxbridge entrants, and sporting success with victory in the prestigious Schools' Cup.

Campbell College had been established very much for the Irish educational market, and regarded itself as *sui generis*. The arrival of R.A.H. MacFarland – an Ulsterman who had taught in an English public school – witnessed the importation of those values of 'muscular Christianity' so prized across the Irish Sea. MacFarland's introduction of the House structure, a prefect system and the Officer Training Corps (OTC) was unpopular with his contemporaries – but they have all survived.

The creation of the OTC, with its Certificate 'A', encouraged 594 boys – at least half the College's register since foundation who were old enough – to enlist in the First World War, in a country in which there was no conscription. One quarter of these – including one who fell victim to the Red Baron – plus one member of staff, gave their lives.

As had his predecessor, MacFarland died in harness, but if he proved retrospectively to be the most unpopular Headmaster, his successor was undoubtedly the most fondly remembered. Fortunately, Col William Duff Gibbon was not deterred by the fact that, acknowledging the unstable political climate, the Governors placed their personal handguns on the table during his interview! He went on to become the longest-serving and undeniably most popular principal in the College's history.

Gibbon had led 9th Battalion the Worcester Regiment into Baghdad during the First World War, and his courage was reflected in the fact that in the 1930s – despite the fact that he had been the most outstanding coach of schoolboy rugby in England – he withdrew Campbell from its premier sporting aspiration, the Schools' Cup, as he felt that it was a distraction from academic goals. Astonishingly, this did not create any apparent legacy of discontent. During his tenure of office the school witnessed expansion in the 1920s with the purchase of three adjacent properties (Cabin Hill, Netherleigh and Ormiston) as Junior and Prep Schools.

Gibbon did not discourage the requisition of the estate as No. 24 General (military) Hospital – a decision which may have proved a blessing when the Luftwaffe, perhaps mistaking it for Stormont, dropped bombs on the building on the night of 4/5 May 1941, killing a number of doctors and patients. The school, with much reduced numbers, had been evacuated in 1940 to the Northern Counties Hotel in Portrush.

Half way through the War, Gibbon surrendered his tenure to Ron Groves who supervised the return to Belmont in February 1946, and refurbished the fabric of the

Aerial view of the school, 1998.

institution after its harsh treatment by the Army. Groves also placed great store on academic attainment and – probably most acceptably in the eyes of many – returned to the Schools' Cup campaign trail, which brought extraordinary success over the next twenty-five years under Bob Mitchell and David Young.

The last half century

The next occupant of the new Headmaster's House in the grounds was the urbane and articulate John Cook. He extended the school's academic success, and his principalship saw an extension of the school buildings, which included the new Sports complex. This era also saw boarding at its peak in Campbell, at marginally under 300. Financial constraints – which had to be regularly tackled from within two decades of the foundation – witnessed the sale of Netherleigh and Ormiston in the 1970s, and some of the proceeds were used to build a new block on the far side of the Parade Ground.

Following a stroke, John Cook took early retirement in 1971. Robin Morgan's period of office was brief, and coincided with the intensification of what became known as 'The Troubles', in which at least seven Campbellians were murdered. Brian Wilson succeeded in 1977, and endeavoured to make a number of bold changes. An annual Arts Week was introduced, Saturday morning teaching was ended and, for the first time in the school's history, girls were enrolled at Sixth Form level. The experiment was accounted a success by all, but was ended after three years by the Department of Education. The decline in boarding numbers – an almost universal feature in Ulster – witnessed a change in the nature of the school, which has adopted a primarily day-boy character.

Following Brian Wilson's resignation in 1987, the Governors made the first internal appointment to the position of Headmaster, when Dr Ivan Pollock was elected. The number of pupils on the Belmont estate is now quadruple its original figure. In the current year, a new block has been built in the Parade Ground, and a dramatically increased enrolment in the last twenty years will be bolstered by the closure of Cabin Hill as a Prep School, and the transfer of all pupils of Year 8 and above to Belmont.

The nature of the book

This volume is designed to reflect the history, activities and character of the College. It also endeavours to provide an insight into the lives and careers of pupils subsequent to their departure from school. A full account of the school's first century can be read in *Neither Rogues nor Fools: a History of Campbell College and Campbellians.*

Although the chapters are self-contained, there is a considerable degree of overlap and flexibility. Within each chapter I have endeavoured to place the images chronologically. I have tried to identify as many individuals as possible; I have not always been successful, due partly to a lack of space, and partly to lapses of memory and the passage of time. With the recent closure of Cabin Hill as a Prep School I felt it appropriate to include images which show something of the adjacent estates and properties once owned by Campbell College.

In a work of this nature, there will inevitably be omissions and gaps. For this I can only apologise. I have endeavoured to be as comprehensive as space allows for over one century of the school's history. School mottoes are needlessly included by the press in any newspaper article about educational establishments; the author is not an enthusiast of them, but such a volume as this does enable us to fulfil that of Campbell College: *Ne Obliviscaris.*

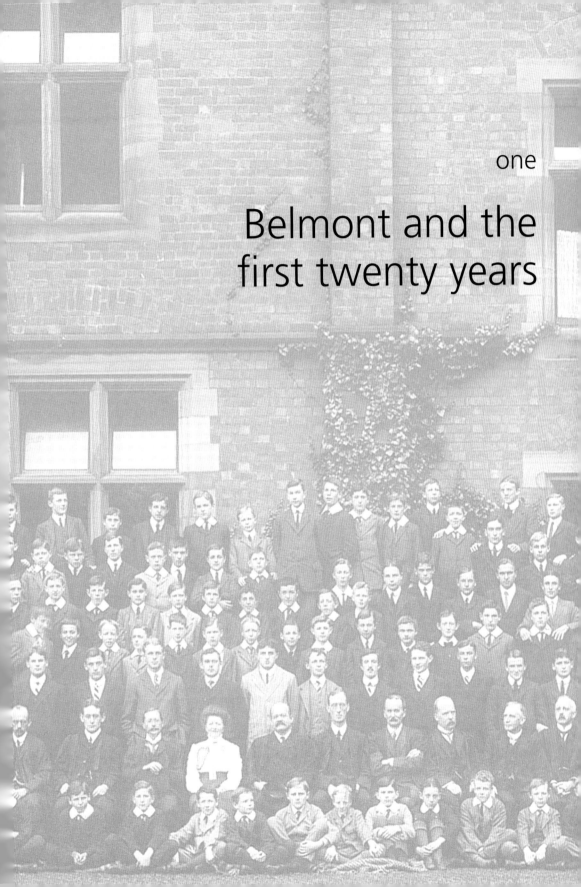

one

Belmont and the first twenty years

Henry Campbell, who died in January 1889, made his fortune supplying the linen trade in the north of Ireland. Unmarried, he granted a few bequests and annuities to family members, and directed that the bulk of his fortune – about £200,000 in contemporary terms – be used for the construction of a hospital or school to bear his name. His Trustees determined on the latter, which was, according to his will, 'to be used as a College for the purpose of giving there a superior liberal Protestant education'.

Joint Headmasters, poached from Methodist College in Belfast, were appointed as early 1890, and one of them – James Adams McNeill – and the architect, William Henry Lynn, toured educational establishments in Great Britain and on the continent in order to adopt the best design features and existing educational practices.

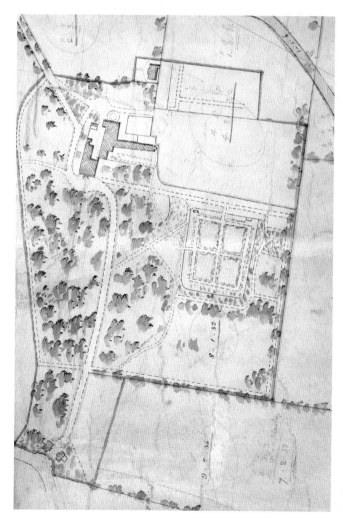

Belmont, the estate of Sir Thomas McClure, was purchased by the Trustees in November 1890 for the site of Campbell College. This detail from McClure's estate map shows the location of Belmont House, at the top of the drive running from the Hawthornden Road. There were three gate lodges, dating from around 1860; only one of these survives and is currently occupied by Brian Robinson, a former Irish rugby international.

The family of Henry Campbell's cousin, and partner at Mossley Mills, John Campbell, *c.* 1887. Two of John's sons – Garrett (in bowler hat) and Howard – were appointed Trustees of Henry's will. Their brother became the future General Sir Walter Campbell, who was mentioned eleven times in despatches during the First World War, and who lost an argument about camels to Lawrence of Arabia.

There have been residents on Belmont estate since the 1750s, such as Richard Brown Bamber and William Bateson. The rather unprepossessing Belmont House may date from the early nineteenth century under the occupancy of solicitor Alexander Montgomery. Thomas McClure, who owned much of the land between the estate and Belfast Lough, was living there by 1860.

Once Belmont was purchased, the old house was apparently used as a Clerk of Works office as the school was built around it from 1891. The latter was not officially completed until 1896, but was regarded as sufficiently ready to open its doors to 215 pupils on 3 September 1894.

Described by one pupil as being like a 'claret-label château', the building and main gate lodge were designed in the Tudor Revival idiom by William Henry Lynn, who also designed the Custom House and Belfast Central Library. The view is nowadays obstructed by extensive planting. The structure, including the gate lodge, is now a listed building, and is shown here in the very early twentieth century. (Reproduced by kind permission of MAGNI).

This view is shown a few years after the previous image. The field is still known as Dickson's Field, after the local nursery dynasty which grew roses in the district. The nearer wing originally formed mirror-image accommodation for the two joint-Headmasters.

Lynn's hammer-beam roof is visible in this early photograph of Central Hall, taken before the addition of the First World War memorial and photographs. The original lighting was gas. There are differences to the current glazing, which suggests that the original glass was replaced as a result of damage caused in the bombing raid on the night of 4/5 May 1941. Pupils sat facing this main window until the installation of the Chapel in 1965.

The Boer War was the first international conflict in which Campbellians participated. J.E. Prentice was killed at Vlakfontein in July 1901, where Lt William John English of 2nd Scottish Horse was pinned down by sixty Boers. As a result of this engagement he became a recipient (age 19) of the Victoria Cross for holding a precarious position. English survived the First World War, and died on 4 July 1941 in command of a troopship. He is buried in Aden. All his medals are shown here.

One of the original pupils, John Hamilton Sinclair went into banking. He fought in the Boer War in 1899, and became known to friends as 'Captain Jack'. He later became a rancher in Canada, but enlisted on the outbreak of the First World War in the Argyll & Sutherland Highlanders. He was mentioned in despatches, was killed in action on 31 October 1916, and is commemorated on the Thiepval Memorial.

In 1903 five school prefects kept a private daily log, rich in sarcasm about the Headmaster, James Adams McNeill. Sunday Church and country walks were the only occasions on which pupils were permitted beyond the perimeter of Belmont estate. This entry was written by Frederick Maurice Wookey who came from Leixlip, Co Dublin. He was mortally wounded near Ypres in March 1915, and is buried in Bailleul Communal Cemetery.

Opposite: These seven members of staff were photographed at the end of the nineteenth century. Seated are (future Professor) Robert Knox McElderry and George Price. The tall central figure is William Allison, and to the right is John Samuels. Leaning casually at the left is Henry Hirsch who in 1904 became Headmaster at Royal School Armagh. The other two have not been identified with certainty.

This is the first photograph, from around 1908, of Yates's House, run by John Yates and (to the right) the diminutive George Thompson. Ten of the twenty-nine boys in this picture perished in the First World War, including both Semple brothers. Two boys became surgeons, two more were missionaries, and another two emigrated to Canada. One became a maltster, and another founded York Rugby Club!

Opposite above: This full school photograph dates to academic year 1910 – 1911. Headmaster R.A.H. MacFarland is flanked by his sister, Mrs Anna Brown, his house-keeper. Virtually all the teaching staff can be seen in the photograph from 1908 (p.22), but only two of the original staff from 1894 had survived: Godfrey Evans (Art) and Dr R.W. Leslie. Standing far left is James Ball, who died on 6 July 1931, after thirty-three years' service as Head Porter.

Standing behind the Headmaster in a frock-coat is Head Prefect Herbert Bartley, later an Inspector-General in the Indian Police. Two to the right, sporting a moustache, is William Fuge who later became a Fellow of the Royal Society of Arts. Between these two is future Regius Professor of Greek, Eric Dodds. Also in the photograph is Arthur Leslie Gregg, the subsequent Head Prefect, who became a noted surgeon and expert in tropical medicine.

The tall boy (4th row back, 6th left), Robert Crichton, was only thirteen, and a future Irish rugby international. This photograph is probably taken in the early part of the academic year, and is unique in that it is the only one in the College Archive to feature the young C.S. Lewis.

Opposite below: This is the first page of the school song, composed about 1910 by John Yates. Boasting such lyrics as 'And win or lose, we play the game' and 'Be true to self and comrades and the school that makes the man', it was clearly influenced by the Victorian concept of 'muscular Christianity', which was imported in 1908 by the new Headmaster, R.A.H. MacFarland, who had taught at Repton.

NE OBLIVISCARIS.

In 1909 Campbell College created the first Officer Training Corps (OTC) at an Irish school. Field Days were conducted, and annual camps in England. This photo was probably taken during the last days of July 1914 at the Farnborough camp which was suddenly curtailed on the outbreak of war. Hugh Gordon is shown third from the left; in addition to working in the public and private sectors, he became the Headmaster's Secretary during the Second World War.

The OTC also instituted an annual Empire Day, at which the Head Prefect planted a tree in the school grounds. In 1914 this ceremony was undertaken by Reginald Cuthbert Whiteside who, on 20 December 1916, was shot down and killed by Manfred von Richthofen, the Red Baron. Also in attendance are the Headmaster (MacFarland), the head gardener and, to the far left (Lt) Henry Staley.

two

The staff

There have been about 300 full-time teaching staff at Campbell College since 1894. Just over ten per cent of these became Headmasters. Female members of staff were a rarity, except in the Art Department, until the 1980s. Now they constitute about one-third of the staff. Some of the staff have been former pupils.

Some staff stayed very briefly, as in the case of Samuel Beckett; the endurance of others has been remarkable. There have been many who have completed over thirty years' service, including Michael McGuffin and John Knox (thirty-six years), Charles Bowen and Theodore 'Taffy' Ragg (thirty-seven), David Young (thirty-nine) and Trevor Carleton (forty). Kenneth Beales (broken by the War) and Raoul Larmour gave forty-two years of teaching service.

This staff photograph was taken in June 1908. Standing are Dr R.W. Leslie, the school doctor; Thomas Dobbin; John Yates; William Pyper; Stephen Bennett, Senior Science Master; C.H. Clarke; Godfrey Evans, Art Master; Corrie Denew Chase, also a noted botanist; and William Baird. Seated are Lewis Alden, whose teaching was acknowledged by four future professors; Robert Davis; the tall William Allison, who taught Mathematics; Headmaster R.A. MacFarland; George Price; Raywood Beaven; and the diminutive George Thompson who, in 1900, became the first former pupil to return as a teacher.

Corrie Chase (right) is pictured near Exeter in 1915 with his parents and brother Bertram. Chase, always known as 'Chevy', was a linguist. He was the first master in charge of the OTC, and enlisted in 1914. He served as a Captain in 16th (Pioneer) Battalion, Royal Irish Rifles, which constructed much of the trench system at the Somme, and was awarded the Military Cross (MC). He started at Campbell in 1905, becoming something of a Mr Chips figure by his death in 1965.

Robert Furley Davis (seated) married in his home town of Nottingham. He was the eponymous founder of the first Day-boy House, and taught Classics from 1902 to 1931. Professor Eric Dodds at Oxford later acknowledged his gratitude to the encouragement of this 'tiny man who wielded the quiet authority of a true scholar'. He died on 14 February 1937, aged 70.

Above: Seven of the staff photographed around 1925. They are Stephen Bennett who, like Chase, was President of the Belfast Naturalists' Field Club; John Yates; Robert Davis; George Price; Corrie Chase; Lewis Alden, whose name now adorns one of the most renowned restaurants in Ireland at Ballyhackamore; and Raywood Beaven. Yates, Davis, Price and Alden – and Allison, who died in 1923 – gave their names to the original Houses.

Right: Raywood Beaven, a mathematician, was the son of a Headmaster of Preston Grammar School and was educated at Westminster School. He was a disciplinarian, and earned the nickname of 'Spitter', but was a Housemaster for many years. Like Chase, he returned in 1939 to help fill teaching gaps caused by the Second World War. His principal interests were rugby and cricket, and he is here caricatured by the future Professor Henry Cronne in his role as rugby referee.

Above: In 1933, the Headmaster, Col William Duff Gibbon (right), visited retired teacher Stephen Bennett at the latter's home in Burslem, in the Potteries, where he had grown up with his cousin, playwright Arnold Bennett. Bennett was a poor disciplinarian, but was a botanical expert, and in 1931 received the coveted Club Medal of the Belfast Naturalists' Field Club. He died on 8 February 1934.

Right: The oldest, most prestigious rugby trophy in Ireland is the Schools Cup, and 1969 Nobel laureate Samuel Beckett played in the 1923 final for Portora against Campbell. Beckett taught at Belmont for two terms in 1928, and quickly determined that it was not the career for him. Beckett is shown here in St Marks' Square, Venice, in the summer of 1927.

Left: This rather dour trio was photographed on Empire Day in the late 1930s. Diminutive Headmaster 'Duffy' Gibbon had been awarded the DSO during the First World War for leading his regiment into Baghdad, and remained a commanding and respected figure. Empire Days remained important to him. He is flanked by a Governor, Canon Crooks (left) – whose OC son, John, became Dean of Armagh – and Malcolm Speir MC, also later on the Board of Governors.

Below left: This photograph was taken in 1941 in the Physics laboratory – an attic – in the Northern Counties Hotel in Portrush, to which Campbell College was evacuated during the Second World War. It shows OC George Taylor, physics teacher, who later became a Schools Inspector. The pupils are I.D. Thompson, A.M. Roulston, D.B. Smith, J.G. Lawson and S.W.H. Kerr, and (seated) W.P. McCaughey (future Governor) and W.J. McDowell.

Opposite above: David Berwick Young (right) – invariably DBY – photographed during the Second World War. He taught English at Campbell from 1948 to 1987; also his coaching, with Bob Mitchell, helped the 1st XV make sixteen appearances in the Ravenhill final in the twenty years to 1970. A memorial stone covers his ashes at Fox's Field, the home of the 1st XV. Pictured also are two friends who travelled to Belfast in 1987 for DBY's appearance on *This Is Your Life*.

Opposite below: Ronald Inge (left) suffered severe spinal injuries in a plane crash in Russia in 1919 which meant he had to wear a back brace for the rest of his life. Despite this, he taught for thirty-two years until 1960, was a Housemaster, and took an active role in running the Campbell (71st East Belfast) Scout unit. He is shown here meeting Chief Scout, Lord Rowallan, at the camp at Ballydrain, 1 and 2 June 1946.

Above: Headmaster Ron Groves (left) watches as his wife, Hilary, curtsies before Princess Margaret and Queen Elizabeth on 1 June 1951. The Royal party had come to Campbell to present the Charter of Incorporation. They are watched by the Very Revd John McKean, Chairman of the Governors, who was soon to become the Presbyterian Moderator. In 1954 Ron Groves was appointed the Master of Dulwich College.

Left: A man of unlimited courtesy and dignity, Albert Maxwell started as a fifteen-year-old at Campbell College in 1929. He saw the R–101 airship fly over the school, and outlasted ten Presidents and thirteen Prime Ministers, finally retiring as Head Porter in 1993 – giving sixty-four years' service! He could recall many pupils' names, and in 1977 was awarded the British Empire Medal. He died on 5 August 1997, and the new timepiece in the Entrance Hall was affectionately named the Albert Clock.

Above: Headmaster John Cook (right) and Chairman of the Governors, Dr R.C. Pink (left), escort Lord Brookeborough – Prime Minister of Northern Ireland (NI) – and his wife to Central Hall for Speech Day on 24 July 1958. Brookeborough used the occasion to support the public and grammar school system, as the school magazine noted, 'in the course of a speech studded with gems of wisdom and art'.

Right: Percy Drake served in the Grenadier Guards. He joined Campbell in 1929 as Instructor with the OTC. He broke his service with the school during the Second World War, enlisting in the Royal Corps of Signals, but returned for a further ten years in 1946. In 1954 he was awarded the British Empire Medal.

Above: Sam Dunlop started teaching when the school was still at Portrush. He was a Housemaster for many years and Vice-Master from 1959 to 1966, before being appointed Headmaster of Belfast High School in the latter year. He is shown here (left) with a group of pupils whom he took to watch the launch of the oil tanker *Harvella* at Harland & Wolff's yard on 26 April 1956.

Left: Cyril Bion had taught in Hong Kong and Mill Hill School before arriving at Campbell as a mathematician in 1923. He gave thirty-one years' service, was an expert in architecture, mechanical drawing and ship design, but is best known as a landscape artist. As this sketch indicates, using the College grounds as inspiration, he was especially interested in trees, and many such works are still in the College's possession.

Above: OC Joe Lytle, Theodore 'Taffy' Ragg and 'Chevy' Chase are photographed probably in the late 1950s, supporting an Allison's House rugby match on Quarry Field. The W.F. Browne Pavilion can be seen in the background.

Right: Peter Evans joined Campbell in 1946, and retired as Vice-Master in 1980. He contributed to the extra-curricular life of the school, notably refusing to call off cricket matches during rain. As a Major in the Combined Cadet Force (CCF), he accompanied the unit in April 1957 to its Easter Camp at Luneberg Heath in Germany. His command of car gears was notorious, so it appears to have been a major act of faith to place him in a tank!

Above: This 1973 photograph shows the staff in Allison's House. In
the same year Tom Garrett (centre) became Headmaster at Portora
and later at RBAI. Alan Bush (left) was awarded the MC at
Arnhem, and was a former Headmaster at Merchiston College. Jack
Ferris later became Headmaster at Down High School. Of the
pupils, M.J. Bion, was a grandson of Cyril Bion, and R.A. Craig
was tragically drowned in 1976.

Right: As female teachers now constitute one third of the staff, it is
clear from this 1976 staff photograph how far its composition has
changed in that time. The tenacity of Mrs Doris McGuffin, left, and
Mme Andrée Knox is noteworthy; they have both survived, whilst
only two of the male staff still haunt the corridors: John Knox and
Dr Ivan Pollock, the current Headmaster.

Robin Morgan (centre), served only five years as Headmaster to
1976, but the other ten teaching staff on the front row totalled 350
years of service between them, including Trevor Carleton (forty
years), Kenneth Beales (forty-two), Raoul Larmour (forty-two) and
David Young (thirty-nine). There are at least ten others featured
who have each given over thirty years' commitment. (The front
row also includes Jim Devlin, Bursar, and OC Denis Acheson,
school doctor). Six in this group – Dr Ivan Pollock, Jack Ferris,
Alan Acheson, Norman Eccles, Tom Patton and Robin Tughan –
went on to become Headmasters.

Right: Brian Wilson arrived at Campbell in 1977 via Radley and Eastbourne College. He was a Classicist with an aptitude for the skills of that ancient era, such as oratory and interpretation of the auspices. He acknowledged the changing times, such as the decline of boarding, and experimented, as with the introduction of Sixth Form girls. During his tenure the facilities were greatly enhanced, including the construction of new laboratories and sporting superstructure.

Left: The maintenance of the school's seventy-acre estate has always been a priority, and a record of the flora and fauna at Belmont was compiled in the 1940s. Tree-planting occurred on each Empire Day, and long service has been acknowledged, as in 1977 and 1998, with mass plantings. On the latter occasion, the compiler of this volume was accorded the honour, but the Headmaster, Dr Ivan Pollock (left), and OC Governor, John Nicholson, proved reluctant to relinquish possession of the tree!

Below: Annual heats and Sports Days require a multitude of personnel at the all-weather track. Pictured here at the finish line are (back row) Mrs Donna Spence, Chris Oswald (partially hidden), Bryan Funston and Jim Hamilton, and Derrick Boyd, Mrs Lynda Haffey (*née* Stewart) and Mrs Wendy Keys. During her career, Lynda has been selected to represent the Ulster Schools, Junior and Senior Hockey squads.

This 1998 staff photograph gives a clearer impression of the increasing number of female staff. In recent years, there has been a more rapid turn-over in staff; six years on, forty per cent of those in this photograph have retired or moved to other posts.

Either side of Dr Pollock are the six members of the contemporary Senior Management Team: Bryan Funston, Michael Caves, Chris Gailey, David Fullerton, Neill Morton (now Headmaster of Portora Royal School) and Joan Dunn (now Mrs McLeod). Three are OCs – Chris Gailey, John Knox and Julian King.

Brian Robinson, towering on the back row, is a former Irish rugby international; to the left is Robin Taylor, who also deputises as a link man and newsreader on Ulster Television.

Left: Over the last few years there have been visits to the First World War battlefields and cemeteries, when graves and memorials relating to former pupils in the war have been visited. There are the names of at least fourteen OCs on the Memorial to the Missing on the Somme at Thiepval, and four former pupils are commemorated on the Menin Gate at Ypres. Photographed here in 2003 at Beaumont-Hamel are Alan Midgley, Alan Stevens and Chris McIvor.

Below: In the summer of 2003 Mathematics and ICT teacher Noel Ashfield (right), along with fifteen others from Northern Ireland, participated in the Habitat for Humanity scheme. He helped to construct seven houses within ten days in El Salvador.

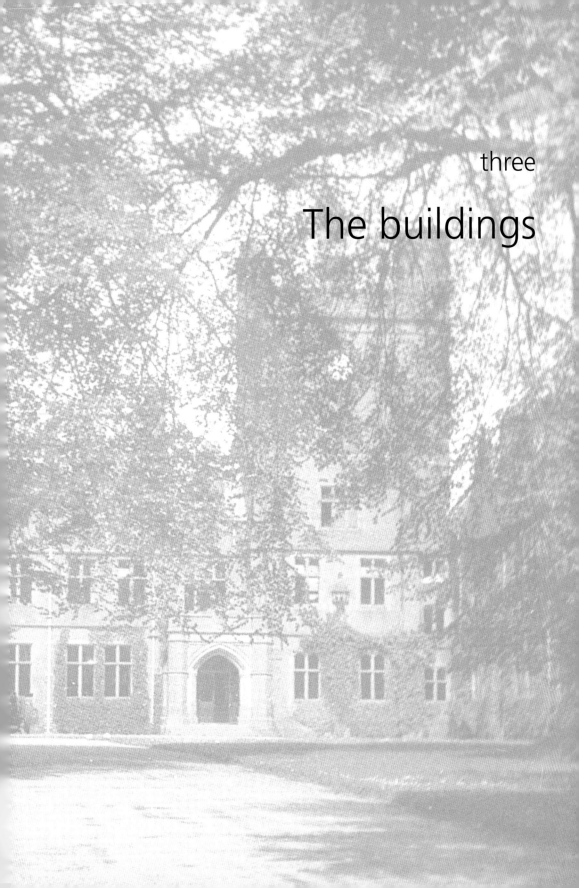

three

The buildings

This chapter presents a number of internal and external views of the College's buildings. Designed by the erstwhile partner of Sir Charles Lanyon, William Henry Lynn, the main school and gate lodge (plus the railings) are now listed buildings. Apart from an additional doorway and the clock in the main tower, the façade differs little from the view which would have greeted the first pupils of September 1894. The south-easterly wing has also lost its bays, with the construction of the Chapel in 1965. Additional buildings have appeared in the grounds, such as The Headmaster's House, the Sports complex, Ormiston and – in 2004 – the new block on the Parade Ground.

Above: This photograph of the front of the College is dated to 1932; the car belonged to Ronald Inge. The façade of Lynn's design has remained virtually unchanged since construction, except for the installation in 1924 of the memorial clock to William Allison. Also just visible is the German field gun presented to the College as a memorial to those Campbellians who served and gave their lives in the First World War.

Opposite above: Upper and Lower Long were originally dormitories that ran the length of the façade above the Dining Hall. Each window illuminated partitioned cubicles, which provided privacy for each boarder. However, the conversion of Campbell into No.24 General Hospital during the Second World War resulted in the military authorities destroying these partitions to create maximum bed space. Upper Long, pictured here, is now the Library; Lower Long is the Sixth Form Centre.

Opposite below: The original cubicles of Upper and Lower Long are shown here as, it would seem, are the fairly primitive washing facilities.

The Entrance Hall was originally decorated with a gasalier and mantle clock taken from Henry Campbell's house, *Lorne*, at Craigavad. The gas lighting was eventually converted to electricity in the 1920s. The nineteenth-century clock bore Henry Campbell's initials (HJC) in filigree chasing, but was stolen in the 1990s. It was replaced by one now called the Albert Clock, in memory of Head Porter Albert Maxwell.

When Campbell opened in 1894, the teaching of science in Ireland was lamentable. James Adams McNeill determined that its provision at the school would be the most advanced, and one of the first pupils – William Caldwell – went on to study at Würzburg University, where x-rays had recently been discovered. This is the Advanced Physics Laboratory (now known as Room 84) probably photographed on the school's return from Portrush.

In the late summer of 1940 Campbell College was evacuated to the Northern Counties Hotel, Portrush, until February 1946. Conditions proved cramped, but it did at least boast an indoor swimming pool, and there were girls in the adjacent Fawcett's Hotel! At least thirteen of the staff enlisted in the Armed Forces, and Corrie Chase and Raywood Beaven – both of whom had officially retired at the end of the 1930s – had to step into the breach.

The former ballroom of the Northern Counties Hotel was used as the school's Assembly Hall. This former railway hotel was destroyed in a malicious fire on 10 March 1990.

During the military occupation of the school, a large number of Nissen huts were erected at the rear of the school. A number were also built in the Parade Ground, and these – shown here in the winter snow of 1950 – continued to be utilised by the school for some years after its return to Belmont. The Nissen Hut on the Parade Ground is the last one in Northern Ireland.

Empire Day, 1951. Behind the CCF unit stands the last remaining gate lodge of McClure's estate, at Hawthornden Road. The lodge was occupied by the family of Billy Hope – Workshop and Pipe Band Instructor – when the IRA raided the College on 27 December 1935, in search of the College Armoury. Three armed IRA men were followed into the lodge by a policeman, and it was fortunate that no-one was killed in the ensuing gunfight in the confined space.

The Dining Hall is photographed – probably in the 1960s – from the Minstrel's Gallery. Used as a cinema during the Second World War, it remains fundamentally unchanged since the opening of the school. The staff's top table sits underneath portraits of the founder, Henry Campbell, and long-serving Headmaster, 'Duffy' Gibbon – the latter painted in 1950 by noted portrait artist, Sir Oswald Birley.

A chemistry class of the 1960s under the eye of Dr Jack Nesbitt, who died suddenly in 1986, as Head of the Department. Jack Nesbitt also organised more off-beat pastimes such as the Beagling Club and, having competed in the Circuit of Ireland rally, the Motor Club.

In the 1960s, in addition to the Prep School, Cabin Hill, Campbell still utilised Netherleigh and Ormiston as junior Houses. Here boys can be seen at the back of the school, completing their trek across from Netherleigh, which passed what in 1966 became Fox's Field.

The Lecture Theatre is one of the original rooms in the College. It has been the venue for such events as a recital by Ralph Vaughan Williams in the 1930s, but its lack of comfort has made it less popular in recent years. In this photograph, Vice-Master Ronnie Caves addresses some Sixth Formers in the early 1980s.

This late 1970s view across the Parade Ground has vanished in the last few months with the construction of the new administrative and classroom block. New temporary classrooms were built over the tennis courts in 1996 to replace those in view which had lasted over twenty years. The sale of Ormiston in 1974 resulted in the construction of a new block bearing the same name – in the far corner – which acted as a junior boarding house and the Technology Department.

Before its present location in the former Upper Long, the school Library used to operate from the first floor of Central Hall. In its earliest days it relied very much upon donations in kind from staff and pupils. The cabinet in the foreground contains a remarkable collection of *lepidoptera* and *araneidae*. The Sixth Form girls in the picture are believed to be Katie Browne and Leigh Robinson.

With the expanding demand of what became known as Craft, Design & Technology, it was determined that a new 'state of the art' Centre should be built at the time of the College's Centenary in 1994. Here Derrick Boyd, Head of Department, is at work with a junior class. Derrick is most versatile with machinery; as one colleague pointed out, 'he is the one person to whom you can lend something, and it will come back in better condition'!

Campbell College

The main school building in around 1998. This was drawn for the College's Christmas card by Graham Acheson, son of another OC, Arthur Acheson, an architect.

four

Ne Obliviscaris

Campbellians have served in most of the major conflicts since the end of the nineteenth century – the Boer War, both World Wars, the Korean War and the Gulf War. Many served in both World Wars although the vast majority, as Irishmen, did not face conscription. The commitment to military service was probably enhanced by the foundation of the Officer Training Corps (OTC) in 1909, which metamorphosed into the Junior Training Corps (JTC) close to the Second World War, and became the Combined Cadet Force (CCF) around 1948.

The first personal sacrifice was J.E. Prentice during the Boer War. About one quarter of the volunteers in the First World War (126 out of 594) gave their life, and about ten per cent (102 out of just over 1,000) in the Second World War. The military graves of Campbellians lie across Europe, Africa and Asia.

Head Prefect Robert Greacen at the flag on Empire Day 1913. Greacen was one of three brothers at Campbell College who hailed from Monaghan. During the First World War he served in various units of the Royal Irish Rifles, sustaining gun shot wounds to his left arm, and to his right leg. After the War he worked as a company representative in Canada, but by the 1980s was back living in Co. Monaghan.

This photograph may have been taken on Field Day operations at Ballygowan on 27 June 1913. The officer in the middle is Capt Corrie Chase, and to the right is Lt Henry Staley. The figure to the left may be Capt Sleeman, an officiating umpire. There is a piper at either end of the group, and the lack of stripes on the uniform of Hugh Gordon – later a Sergeant – suggests that this photograph was taken in 1913.

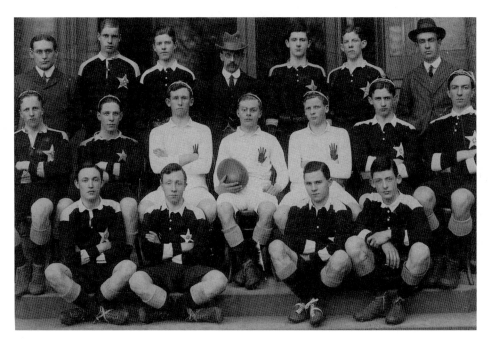

The camaraderie of the 1914 1st XV squad was destroyed by the First World War. Seven of them did not survive the war, and two of them also lost another brother during the conflict. Robert Semple was killed only six days before the Armistice; and the team captain – R.C. Whiteside – died at the hands of the Red Baron. One of the staff, William Madden (top right), was also killed in March 1918.

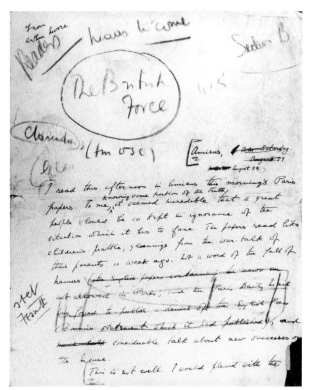

The Amiens Despatch, published in *The Times* on 30 August 1914, was the first authentic report of military action in the First World War. It told of the disastrous retreat from Mons, and caused a furore in Parliament, in the Press, and amongst the public, who felt that it was untrue and disloyal to the war effort. It was written by *Times* reporter and OC Arthur Moore, who had recently arrived in France after reporting events in Albania.

The Pipe Band, *c.* 1914–1915 by the sister of E.T. Dobson, one of those in the next photograph. One or two of those marching are seen in the 1916 posed photograph on the next page.

In this 1915 OTC photograph, there are two unit Sergeants seated each side of the Headmaster, Mr MacFarland, who throughout the War ignored complaints from the pupils about hardships by urging 'Remember the men in the trenches'.

The four Sergeants were R.Y. Crichton, later an Irish rugby international; J.V. Collins, who took up market gardening and farming, and was awarded the OBE; Hugh Gordon, who features elsewhere in this book; and E.T. Dobson, who served in the 74th Punjabis, and died as a member of 2/124th Baluchistan Infantry in tragic circumstances at Alexandria on 8 June 1920.

Above: The 1916 OTC Pipe Band features J.H. Bewglas, later a Presbyterian Minister; J.H.L. Stewart; B.O. Smith; W.H. Smith, later in the Colonial Medical Service; A.R. Gilchrist, appointed to the Royal College of Physicians; and (front row) A.J. Emerson; A.D. Macnamara, later in the Indian Army, and awarded the DSO and OBE; T.S.S. Fleming, who joined Dominion Gramophone Records Ltd; and G.L. Craig, who joined the Army.

Left: This plaque to Henry Ouseley Davis is in Holywood Parish Church. Leaving Campbell in 1903, he made a career in the Army, following in the footsteps of his great-grandfather, General Sir Ralph Ouseley. In 1913-1914 he served on the HQ Staff of the Ulster Volunteer Force about a mile from the school at Craigavon. H.O. Davis was the second Campbellian to die in the trenches, a victim of shrapnel wounds.

Above left and above: Robert (Robin) MacDermott was the middle son of Revd Dr John MacDermott, a Campbell Governor and minister at Belmont Presbyterian Church. He was qualifying as a barrister when he enlisted in 8th Battalion Royal Irish Rifles. He was killed by a shell on 8 January 1916, becoming the first battalion officer of 36th (Ulster) Division to die. Second Lt MacDermott now lies in plot I.A.30 at Auchonvillers Cemetery. His younger brother, Clarke, later became Lord Chief Justice of Northern Ireland.

Left: There had long been close links between the textile trade in the north of Ireland and Belgium, and when Jerome Lennie Walker left Campbell in 1905 he went to work for his father's company in Courtrai. When his family fled the German advance in 1914, he stayed in Belgium, working with the Red Cross. He enlisted in 14th Battalion Royal Irish Rifles, and was killed in action on 6 May 1916. He is buried in Authuille Cemetery (plot I.D.58).

Right and below: Leaving Campbell in 1900, Edmund de Wind worked in banking. Emigrating in 1911, he worked for the Canadian Bank of Commerce, but enlisted on the outbreak of the war. Initially in the Canadian forces, he obtained a commission in the Royal Irish Rifles in 1917. He was on the front line near St Quentin when the Germans launched their final assault on 21 March 1918, and was posthumously awarded the Victoria Cross for the gallant defence of his position. Edmund's name is commemorated on this plaque at the Ulster Tower near Thiepval, and he features on the banner of Comber LOL no.100. There is also a mountain named in his honour in Alberta, Canada.

Above and above right: Dubliner Maurice Lea Cooper left Campbell in the summer of 1914. In April 1917 he joined the Royal Naval Air Service, amalgamated a year later to form the RAF. Cooper was promoted to Captain with 213 Squadron, and became the first Irishman to win the Distinguished Flying Cross (DFC). He was killed, aged nineteen, after being hit during a raid, and is buried in Dadizeele New British Cemetery (plot 6.B.40).

Right: John Boyers came to Campbell from Longford, and qualified – like ten per cent of all Campbellians – as a doctor. He joined the Royal Army Medical Corps (RAMC), but contracted pneumonia whilst tending the survivors of SS *Leinster*, sunk by a U-boat on 1 October 1918, and died just over three weeks later. He lies buried in the family plot at St Ann's Church at Newtown Forbes in Co. Longford. St Ann's minister was the father of OC W.F. Browne.

Above: Robert Lloyd Thompson lived at Penrhyn, now the Prep School of Strathearn. He adopted his father's trade of a fancy linen manufacturer. He became a Major in the Royal Field Artillery, being twice mentioned in despatches and was awarded the Military Cross in 1917. His family installed this commemorative window in St Mark's Church at Dundela, after he was killed at the Battle of Cambrai on 1 December 1917.

Right: The only full-scale Speech Day during the First World War was held in July 1917. The pupils accepted certificates instead of the usual prize money, which was donated to the Public Schools Hospital. This certificate was awarded to J.R.H. Greeves who became a Director of several companies, and President of the Linen Hall Library in Belfast. He was a Governor of the College from 1950 for over twenty years.

Below: Empire Day and its tree-planting ceremony continued throughout the First World War and beyond. This photograph shows the occasion in May 1919 when the tree was planted by Head Prefect, R.A.J. Somers. His brother, Second Lt C.D. Somers, had died of wounds in France on 20 April 1917, and he himself died on active service in Burma in the Indian Army in December 1941 – one of four Campbellian families to lose a son in each of the World Wars.

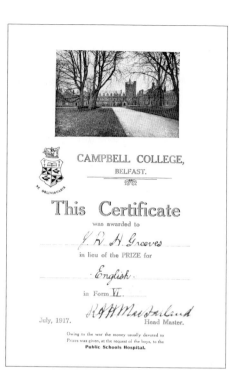

CAMPBELL COLLEGE,
BELFAST.

This Certificate
was awarded to

J. R. H. Greeves

in lieu of the PRIZE for

English.

in Form *VI.*

July, 1917.   Head Master.

Owing to the war the money usually devoted to Prizes was given, at the request of the boys, to the **Public Schools Hospital.**

Opposite below, left and right: Lt-Col Frederick Bradley adopted medicine as his profession and worked in India. He joined the RAMC during the First World War. He was the inventor of a delousing machine, and was awarded the DSO in January 1918. Killed by a shell whilst asleep in a dug-out a few weeks before the end of hostilities, he was buried at Barastre, near Bapaume in France. In April 2004 his great-grandson, Matthew Bradley, paid tribute with a memorial cross at his grave.

Above: The German field gun, photographed here in 1932, was presented to the College in 1923 as a tribute to the contribution of Campbellians in the First World War. It graced the front of the school until 1940 when, like so much else, it was taken away to be melted down in the seemingly vain hope of trying to provide scrap metal for the new war effort.

Below: This photograph shows the *feu de joie* in the Parade Ground on Empire Day 1937, following the planting of sixteen beech trees and one oak on the path to the Sanatorium. The chief guest was OC John Archer, Town Clerk of Belfast.

Right: The OTC was established before the First World War to provide officers for the British Expeditionary Force. It was considered appropriate to undertake such training in Public Schools, and those who passed the various facets of training were awarded Certificate 'A', and could enter the Army at Officer rank. This certificate was awarded in 1924 to Walter Paul, who was CSM of the OTC, and ultimately joined the Colonial Administrative Service.

Below: Shooting has been an integral feature of the OTC and CCF. Campbell College first entered the prestigious Ashburton Shield at Bisley in 1929, and recently the teams have won as many trophies as the other sports combined! Featured is the 1930 Shooting squad. With Capt Charles Bowen are E.A.S. Brett, -?-, -?- and W.H. McGiffin. Seated are R.W.G. Charlesson, -?-, G.T. Farley, -?- and H.L.McL. Bulloch. George Farley was killed by the bomb at the King David Hotel in Jerusalem on 22 July 1946. The names of the two boys seated on the ground are unknown.

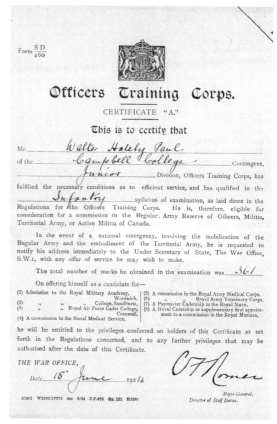

One of the main pioneers of The Toc H movement in Ireland was OC William Armour, editor of *The Northern Whig*. It was introduced to Campbell College in 1933 as a means of introducing senior boys to the idea of service in the local community. In this photograph a group of Campbellians with Charles Bowen visits Talbot House, Toc H's inspirational centre, at Poperinghe (near Ypres) in August 1938.

OTC camps continued regularly during the 1930s. Here at Strensall in Yorkshire in 1937, manoeuvres are taking place between companies on a Field Day. During the night, Campbell units waited for an attack which failed to materialise.

The OTC unit arrives at Strensall station on 27 July 1935. The cadet looking at the camera, second from right, is Desmond Hughes. 'Hawkeye' was one of the most successful pilots during the Second World War, with eighteen and a half kills. He had command of No.604 (Mosquito) squadron, became Commandant of Cranwell, and rose to the rank of Air Vice Marshal. Awarded the CB, CBE, DSO, DFC + two bars and AFC, he died on 11 January 1992.

Campbell cadets form the Brigade Guard at Strensall in 1937. The bugler is George Dougan, later a doctor and High Sheriff of Armagh. In the front rank are Sergeant W.A. Edmenson, killed in action in 1940; J.F. Yates; and James Calvert, who served in the 8th Army. The sentry is John Fleming. In the rear rank are Cpl J.B.H. Martin, later a doctor, Basil Tweedie, Edwin Graham, and David Stuart.

In 1939 Campbell College viewed the prospect of war very seriously. Gas masks, fire appliances and first-aid kits were purchased and, as in the First World War, provision was made on the estate for food production. Additionally, on the back drive, five air-raid shelters were constructed, which could accommodate fifty individuals each.

During the Second World War Campbell College was transformed into No.24 General (military) Hospital. These four men, one of whom was named Syd, are believed to have belonged to the RAMC. They are photographed at the Hawthornden Road gate lodge in August 1941.

Top: On the night of 4/5 May 1941 the Luftwaffe made its second raid over Belfast. Bombs were dropped along the Belmont Road, some falling on Campbell College, which was perhaps mistaken for nearby Stormont. Damage was caused to the roof at the corner of one of the northern wings. As a military hospital, Campbell received priority from the Fire Brigades, and other properties in the district, such as Clonallon, burned to the ground.

Above: Bomb damage was also caused to Nissen Hut wards at the rear of the school, and almost a score of patients and doctors were killed in the raid.

During the war the links between the school and the town of Portrush were consolidated, and the College Pipe Band, under the leadership of Pipe Major Dennis Carson, led the VE Day parade through the coastal town on 8 May 1945.

Fifty years later to the day, the Campbell Pipe Band participated in the 50th anniversary celebrations. Pictured here on the sea-front at Portrush are: Andrew Dowdall, Michael Orr, Nathan Kohner, Neil McCarroll, Christopher Johnston, Sam Ballard and Grant Boyd; kneeling are Jason Douglas, John Hope, James Kyle, William Walker, Derek Young and Michael Neill.

Top: The CCF parade on a wet 1951 Empire Day indicates that there was also a good turn-out by parents. The staff taking the salute include Bob Mitchell (RN) and Kenneth Beales and Peter Evans (Army). In the distance is Corrie Chase, who was the first Captain of the OTC, and would have been present at the first Campbell Empire Day parade.

Above: A CCF march past in the 1950s led by Major Peter Evans, who had served as a lieutenant in the Royal Artillery in the Second World War and had been mentioned in despatches.

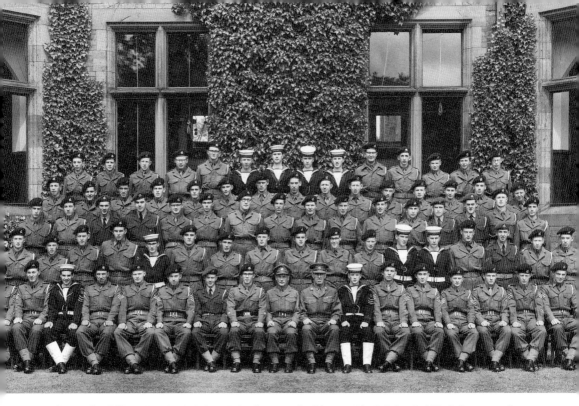

Above: The full 1960 CCF NCO unit is photographed here with OC Lt-Col Ted Garrett and RSM Harry Bradshaw. On the front row is Derry Whyte, Hon Secretary of the OC Society, and Paddy Hughes, elder son of Air Vice Marshal Desmond Hughes, who has won international awards for his films. In the Navy uniform, to the right of Harry Bradshaw, is Peter Gibson QC, a County Court Judge. Also on the front row are John Collins, future Chairman of Shell, and Patrick Freeman who supplied the photograph.

Mike Gibson (brother of Peter) and Freddie Craig – who were to be opposing captains in the 1965 Varsity march – also appear, as does Iain Johnstone, well-known author and film critic of *The Sunday Times*, who co-wrote (with John Cleese) *A Fish Called Wanda II*. Future Head Prefect Damian Cranmer, later Director of Music at the Guildhall School of Music and Drama can also be seen.

Many were to carve out successful careers in the public and private commercial world. These included George Boyle, John Turner, John Hawthorne, William Baird, George Adams and Alexander Shooter, whose father wrote *Ulster's Part in the Battle of the Somme*. Some have since emigrated to Canada.

Opposite above: A group of Campbellians become acquainted with a tank at the Easter 1957 CCF camp near Luneberg Heath. The group includes Chris Gailey, John Green, Ian Irwin, Scott Buchanan, Hugo Curry and Brian Bolton.

Opposite below: The Governor of Northern Ireland, Lord Wakehurst, inspects the Pipe Band on the occasion of the Jubilee of the OTC/CCF on 30 May 1959. He was also presented to Corrie Chase, the original commanding officer of the OTC. The Hon ADC of Lord Wakehurst was OC John Higginson CBE, who was also a founder of the Manor Street Boys' Club (in North Belfast), sponsored by the College.

Above: The Pipe Band, 8 p.m., 5 April 1995. Led by Drum Major Neil McCarroll, the band comes to attention in Meensestraat for the Last Post ceremony at the Menin Gate in Ypres.

Right: (Left to right) Buglers Michael Shanks, Andrew Fullerton, Ryan Richardson, Garth Funston and Nicholas McKimm line up at Speech Day in the late 1990s.

Opposite above: Apart from his teaching and Housemaster responsibilities, Bob Mitchell's main interests were coaching rugby and leading the RN section of the CCF. Here he is pictured in 1958 supervising a knot-tying demonstration, which includes M.B.N. Butler (kneeling), D.C. Neill, George Adams and R.O.W. Wormell. Bob Mitchell, who lived on an island in Strangford Lough, retired in 1973 to the south of England.

Opposite below: CCF members enter one of the helicopters that graced the impressive CCF Centenary military tattoo at Belmont on 13 May 1994, organised by Lt-Col Denis Grant OBE.

David Russell, then aged thirteen, who became a world champion piper in his teens, plays in the main square at Péronne in France, April 1995.

The Duke of Westminster inspects the CCF in front of the College on 19 March 2004, accompanied by Pilot Officer Michael Jackson.

five

Playing the game of life

*I*n the late nineteenth-century, public schools, following Rugby's Thomas Arnold, adopted a social discipline which became known as 'muscular Christianity', expressed most concisely in Sir Henry Newbolt's rallying cry of 'Play up, and play the game'. The virtues and ideals learned at school – such as duty, perseverance, courage and integrity – were expected to be good training for life, particularly for service in the British Empire. Such idealism was reinforced at Campbell when MacFarland arrived as Headmaster from Repton in 1908. John Yates, in composing the school song in 1910, incorporated this philosophy in such lines as: 'As we played the game at Campbell, so we'll play the game in life'.

Left: George Mitchell came second in the Indian Army entrance examination, and served on the North West Frontier. Wounded in 1916, he was killed, aged twenty, whilst a member of 45th Rattray's Sikhs on 1 February 1917, during the attack on Kut in Mesopotamia (now Iraq). He is buried at the Amara War Cemetery in Iraq.

Right: George Mitchell's younger brother, Frederick Julian, left Campbell in 1919. He was successively rector at Finaghy and Ballymena. In 1950 he was elevated to the episcopate at Kilmore, Elphin and Ardagh, and was translated to Down and Dromore in 1955. He died in June 1979.

Above: Arthur Moore, later an international journalist and editor, left Campbell in 1900 and, despite an obscure personal background, was elected President of the Oxford Union in 1904 (in which office he was followed by fellow OCs William Armour in 1907 and James Brown in 1937). He is shown here (seated centre) outside the Union building.

Left: Whilst Victorian travellers had visited the extremes of Albania, it was in 1908 that Arthur Moore claimed to be 'the first west European to penetrate central Albania'. In thrall to the blood-feud, the country was extremely dangerous, and Moore needed an armed guard. One of the people he met in Bourgayet was a thirteen-year-old boy, who was later to become King Zog of Albania.

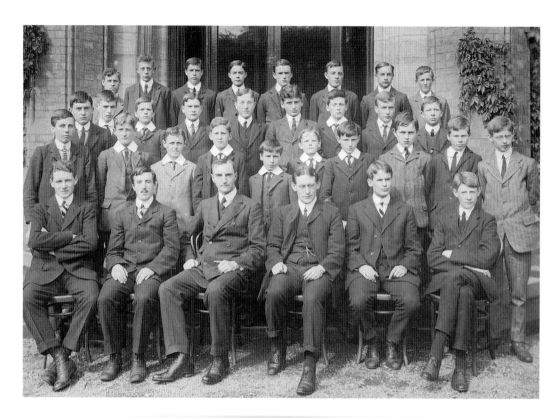

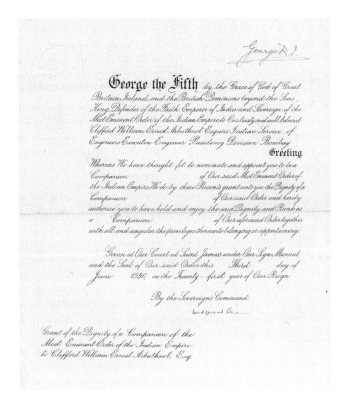

Above left: Over three per cent of pre-Second World War OCs travelled to India to find employment. Many were decorated for their service, including C.W.E. Arbuthnot, who was awarded the CIE in June 1930. Originally an engineer, he served on Public Service Commissions, and became Rent Controller of Bombay for 1942–1947. His CIE certificate was signed by the Secretary of State for India, William Wedgwood Benn, father of Tony Benn.

Above right: Thomas Dunlop (top) and John Kelly played together in the 1st XV in 1902. Kelly joined the Government of India, and became Controller of Currency in Calcutta in 1932. He was awarded the CIE in 1934. Dunlop entered the Consular Service and served in various locations, becoming Consul for New Caledonia in the Pacific. He was knighted in June 1939, having done much to improve working conditions in the Service.

Opposite above: This photograph of 1911 shows Mr Yates with a different assistant – Henry Staley – to that on page 18. Six of these boys died in the First World War, including Robert, son of the jeweller, Sharman Neill. Typical of Campbellians, they worked around the globe in such locations as Nigeria, China, Argentina, Ceylon and India. There are six pairs of brothers, including the Clarke brothers. Stewart Clarke, an Oxford scholar, drowned at Salamis on 3 May 1924, and Brice helped to eradicate tuberculosis from the north of Ireland.

Opposite below: James Samuel Davidson, one of the first pupils at Campbell, became Managing Director of his father's company, Sirocco Works, on whose behalf he undertook a round-the-world voyage in 1910–1911. He joined the Ulster Volunteer Force in 1913, enlisted in the Royal Irish Rifles, and was killed on the first day of the Battle of the Somme. He is pictured here as a member of the Royal Ulster Yacht Club, where he sailed his yacht, *Iris*.

Above: Charles Bartley, a Schools Inspector, sent three of his six sons to Campbell College. They all pursued careers in India. Here seen at the wedding of brother Herbert in Calcutta in January 1926, John (left) served in the Indian Civil Service for thirty-five years. He was awarded the CIE and CSI, and was knighted in 1945. Frederick (middle) won the King's Police Medal (KPM) twice. Herbert became an Inspector General in the Indian Police, also won the KPM, and was awarded the CIE in 1947.

Right: The son of a minister at Newtown Forbes, Co. Longford, William Fraser Browne was known to his friends as 'Horsey'. He played for the 1st XV for three years, captaining the squad in 1921 – when he was also Head Prefect. He went to Sandhurst, played rugby for the Army, and won twelve caps for Ireland between 1924 and 1927. Browne died of leukaemia on 23 May 1931 at the age of twenty-eight. On 18 October 1932, with a match played against an international team, the new pavilion was named in his honour.

Left: Pictured at Pinewood Studios, William MacQuitty left Campbell in 1923. He spent his early years in banking in India. On returning home, he found a niche in the British film industry, responsible for such productions as *A Night to Remember*, about the sinking of RMS *Titanic*. He founded Ulster Television, created the forerunner of the Open University and was an outstanding photographer, noted for his picture of the funerary mask of Tutankhamun and for *Persia: the Immortal Kingdom*. He died on 5 February 2004, aged ninety-eight.

Below: John Yates was Housemaster to some remarkable pupils. He is shown here in 1922 with yet another assistant, Victor Harper, who later that year became Headmaster at Lurgan College. Amongst the pupils here are Eric Megaw and William MacQuitty. Others include Haddon Common, future Professor of Agricultural Chemistry in Montreal, and H.C.M. Stone, who worked in the British Embassy in Washington DC.

This plaque at Queen's University's Ashby Institute is to Eric Megaw, one of four remarkable Campbellian brothers. Intrigued by radio whilst at school, Megaw intercepted the first radio signal received in Ireland from New Zealand. He later experimented with short-wave radio, and demonstrated his apparatus at lectures by Marconi. His work proved critical to the development of radar in the Second World War. Awarded the MBE in 1943, he died in January 1956, aged only forty-eight.

The OC Society established a London Branch. Headmaster 'Duffy' Gibbon attended the one shown here, held on 8 February 1935. One of those who attended regularly at this period was Freeman Wills Crofts (top table, 3rd left – next to George Price). Originally an engineer on the Belfast & Northern Counties Railway, Crofts took up writing during an illness, and became most celebrated for his Inspector French detective novels. He died on 11 April 1957.

William Scott was one of the original members of the OTC. During the First World War Captain Scott was twice mentioned in despatches, and in 1917 earned both the MC and DSO, to which was later added a bar. A wartime jacket, bearing two serious lacerations, is on show at a museum in Armagh. He remained a military man, and was the only victim of a random air-raid on a hotel in Arras during the Second World War.

Commander Nigel Pelly clocked up over 2 million air miles in the RAF and civil aviation. During the Second World War he established the Desert Supply service in West Africa, and was awarded the OBE in 1944. He was Director of Operations during the 1948 Berlin Airlift, but is perhaps best remembered as the pilot who flew Chamberlain to Munich to meet Hitler at Berchtesgaden in September 1938.

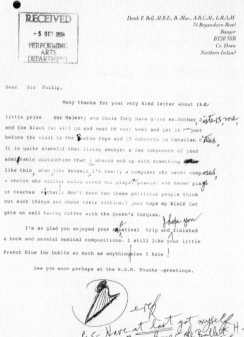

Derek F. Bell, M.B.E., B. Mus., A.R.C.M., L.R.A.M.
74 Bryansburn Road
Bangor
BT20 5SB
Co. Down
Northern Ireland

Dear Sir Philip,

Many thanks for your very kind letter about the little prize. Her Majesty and Uncle Tony have given me. Mother sisters me, and the Black Cat will go and meet HM next week and get it — just before the visit to the Boston Pops and 15 concerts in Canadian cities. It is quite shameful that living amongst a few composers of your admirable distinction that I should end up with something else like this, when like Henselt I'm really a composer who never composed, a oboist who neither makes reeds nor plays, pianist who never plays or teaches either! I don't know how these political people think out such things and chose their victims. I just hope my BLACK Cat gets on well having coffee with the Queen's Corgies.

I'm so glad you enjoyed your sabbatical trip and finished a book and several musical compositions. I still like your little French Blue for Dublin as much as anything else I know! I hope you

See you soon perhaps at the R.S.M. Thanks — greetings,

Derek

P.S. Have at last got myself the CDs of Ring, Roger the Ballet H. 4 Symphs. of 50 Mozarteas, fiddle conc, very fine music indeed

Above: Squadron Leader Terry Bulloch probably flew more hours than any other wartime pilot, and was by far the most outstanding anti-submarine air ace of the Second World War with four destroyed and severe damage to two others. He brought the first Flying Fortresses across the Atlantic, and flew Liberators (beside which he is photographed here) in 120 Squadron of Coastal Command. His achievements are reflected in the award of a DSO + bar and DFC + bar.

Left: As this letter regarding his MBE to fellow OC Philip Hammond suggests, Derek Bell was a unique and unorthodox character. He was an outstanding virtuoso and improviser on several instruments. In addition to several solo records, he also made albums with Van Morrison, Sir James Galway and Mick Jagger, although he is possibly best known as the harpist with the Chieftains. His death on 16 October 2002 created an irreplaceable void in the Irish music scene.

Above: Four OCs are reunited at the Cabin Hill reunion, 10 April 2003. Pictured are (left) Terence Mack, Administrator at Castle Ward, and (right) Professor Ronnie Buchanan OBE, recent NI Chairman of the National Trust, and first Director of the Institute of Irish Studies. Framed by these two are (left) Dr Max Wright, Senior Lecturer in Philosophy at QUB – who was sent to Campbell after the Luftwaffe dropped a bomb on his home! – and Chartered Surveyor Peter Fair.

Left: Professor Emeritus James Stevens Curl is one of the most outstanding scholars that Campbell has produced. In addition to his countless papers, articles and reviews, he is the author of numerous acclaimed books, including *The Londonderry Plantation 1609-1914*, *The Victorian Celebration of Death* and, in preparation, *The Egyptian Revival*, plus other volumes on Victorian, Classical and Georgian architecture, as well as the standard *Oxford Dictionary of Architecture*. He has been the recipient of many awards, and lectures nationally and internationally.

Above: Four of the five members of the group The Dominoes – photographed here in 1962 – were Campbellians: Roderick Downer on drums, Dick Pentland (not an OC) on saxophone, Fred Isdell, Mike Shanks and Bill Morrison. All with other professional careers, they performed over the years at various functions at the College, but were widely known throughout the province, following heady days on a tour with Roy Orbison. Very sadly, Fred Isdell passed away in recent months.

Left: The son of an OC, Chris Gailey was a former pupil who returned to teach history and politics for over thirty years. He was a highly-respected Housemaster, who made a considerable contribution to the extra-curricular life of the College, in the CCF and the sporting world. He is featured here as Field Marshal Sir Douglas Haig in the 1994 production of *Oh! What a Lovely War*. He retired as Vice-Master in 1998.

Above: Pictured here in 1988 with Danny La Rue and Linda Nolan (of the Nolan sisters), Gordon Burns presents *Password*, one of many TV programmes with which he has been associated. Leaving school in 1960, he began his career with *The Belfast Telegraph*. He then became a sports presenter with Ulster TV, and eventually moved to Granada. Now a freelance broadcaster, he is best known for creating and hosting *The Krypton Factor*.

Right: Dr Philip Hammond, Arts Development Director at the Arts Council of Northern Ireland, is shown working at his composition French Blue. Philip obtained the first doctorate of music at Queen's University Belfast to be awarded by submission. He was formerly Director of Music at the Prep School, Cabin Hill. His composition *Waterfront Fanfares* was the first piece of music to be played in the Waterfront Hall at Laganside in Belfast. He is also a regular broadcaster on BBC Radio 3 and local radio.

'Honest, Ted, they're not mine!' In 1996 whilst still at school, Andrew – son of Biology teacher David Fullerton – won a role as Philip Nugent in Neil Jordan's film *The Butcher Boy*. He is pictured here (left) with Alan Boyle, who played Joe, and Ardal O'Hanlon, star of *Father Ted*. Andrew is currently pursuing his long-time ambition to qualify as a vet.

Above and right: Since leaving Campbell in 1981, John Irvine has enjoyed an outstanding career in journalism. He cut his teeth on *The Tyrone Constitution*, and worked at Ulster TV from 1987 – 1994. He then became the Ireland correspondent for ITN, and has since proceeded to become their Middle Eastern Correspondent. He gained fame as the first reporter to greet American troops arriving in Baghdad in 2003. He currently resides in Thailand.

six

Occasions and pastimes

*I*n over a century of existence, the College has hosted a multitude of events – indoor and outdoor – which are frequently open to the parents and public. Also, the extra-curricular activities (apart from on the sports fields) have been diverse and even exotic! Some have proved transient, others have proved resilient and enduring. Most of them reflect the zeitgeist. Although treated with a mixture of mirth and admiration, the Wireless Society, under the genius of Eric Megaw, was fashionable in the 1920s; by the 1980s the Doctor Who Society, under the zealous leadership of Robert Simpson, proved more topical.

The date of this visit of Sir James and Lady Craig to Campbell College is uncertain. They had lived at Craigavon on Circular Road close to the school, and there were very close links between the house and the College during the Home Rule Crisis, 1912-1914. The Northern Ireland Government Cabinet offices were located at Cabin Hill during the early 1920s. Sir James attended the OTC's twenty-first anniversary dinner on 30 October 1930.

Three Scouts – T.B. Dunn, J.K.L. Houston and (on the rope bridge) C.T.B Adams – take it easy at Ormiston lake in the summer of 1932. The latter two became surgeons and physicians; Thomas Dunn was a future Governor of the College and President of the OC Society.

The Junior Dramatic Society play on 27 March 1934 was *A Midsummer Night's Dream*. It featured (not in order): F.K. Austin, W.A. Edmenson, J.B.A. Miller, C.D.G. Shaw, J.D.R. McCullagh, T.B. McVicker, A.T. Boyle, A.W. Pringle, L.S. Orr, J.E. Pyper, T.M. Roulston, D.B. Kenny, R.B. McDowell, I.V. Watson, C. Grainger, W.G. McNeill, F.D. Hughes, W.E.B. Atkinson, J.T. Shepherd, G.A. Waters, D.H. Cronne and S. Storey.

Above: The 71st (East Belfast) Scouts attend summer camp at Shane's Castle, 1948. From left to right, back row: J.W.McC. Miller, J.R.S. Phillips, B.W.A. Tyrrell, Mr R.M. Inge and R.A. Ledlie. Middle row: G.S. Claney, J.H. Allport, W.F. Madden, R.A. Bailey, I.A.P. Scott, A.A. Craigie and D.H. Capper. Front row: L.B. Archibald, P.G. Weir, ? Carson, J.E. Parr, T.F. Muldrew, J.M. McKelvey, R.H. Dinsmore and S.S. Frackelton.

Below: Major Joe Lytle escorts HM Queen Elizabeth as she reviews the Guard of Honour during her visit to the College on 1 June 1951.

Above: The Pipe Band still performs on Speech Days for the chief guest and visitors, but the large tree and the marquees – seen here probably in the 1950s – have disappeared from the scene in recent years.

Below: The buglers of the Pipe Band play in Main Street, Bangor on 12 February 1952, to celebrate the accession of Queen Elizabeth II. The fanfare was composed by Captain Kenneth Beales who was a musician in addition to being Head of the Mathematics Department.

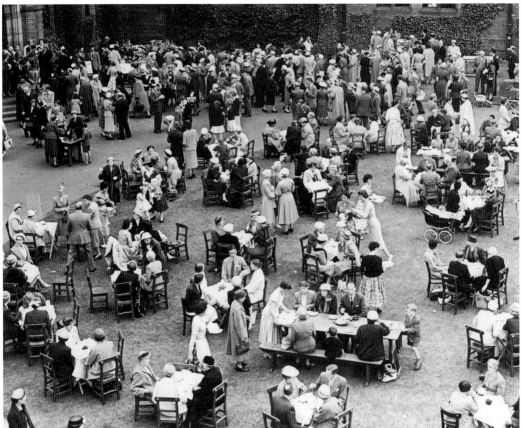

Above: In the early 1960s the Scouts constructed a robust log bridge across Ormiston lake.

Right: One of the more unusual activities, encouraged by Dr Jack Nesbitt, was beagling. It is believed (if not with absolute certainty) that these four pupils are being introduced to the technicalities of this pastime.

Opposite above: For many decades there have been some outstanding dramatic productions in the Central Hall, including some of plays by the former member of staff Samuel Beckett. The featured production was of Shakespeare's *Henry IV Part 1* in the late 1950s.

Opposite below: This fête, opened by Lady Wakehurst, the wife of the Governor of Northern Ireland, was held on 1 June 1957. It was claimed that over 3,000 people attended, and the CCF Pipe Band took the opportunity to parade its new uniform. The long benches are still functional in the Dining Hall nearly half a century later!

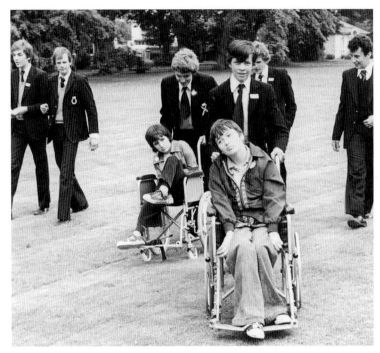

The Social Services group was created in the 1960s by Fred Parkes. There were many visits to local residential homes, and much work was done with handicapped children through the PHAB organisation. Here, in around 1981, in the grounds of neighbouring Strathearn school, Campbell boys entertain pupils from Fleming Fulton. The boys include David Bevan, Nigel Duffield and Kimon Catechis.

Linked with the Duke of Edinburgh Award scheme was Adventure Training in the Mournes. Here in around 1983/84 are Paul Donald (right) and Philip Rogers (centre). Philip was raised in Little Lea, the house in which C.S. Lewis had lived on Circular Road.

David Catherwood's first jazz band in around 1983. It was comprised of Robert Bell, Peter Greeves, Robert Porter, Michael Wray, Patrick Logan and Paddy Boyd.

In 1988 former Page Three girl Linda Lusardi won first prize in a competition for a big night out with five Campbellians: Rory Collins, Gareth McGimpsey and Jackson Collins, and (front) Ian Feely and Gavin Clarke.

David Fullerton plays General Lanrezac, who shows disdain for Field Marshal Sir John French, played by OC Julian King in the 1994 production of *Oh! What a Lovely War*. David has been Head of the Biology Department since 1981 and on the Senior Management Team since 1987. After a period on the staff at Campbell, Julian has recently moved to teach Classics at Belfast High School.

In the early 1990s the school quiz team of Scott Kennedy, Paul Stephens, Neil Miller and James Brown meet local TV personality, Gerry Kelly.

On 16 May 1995 Sir Patrick Mayhew, Secretary of State for Northern Ireland, addressed the school's Sixth Form on the subject of political progress in the province. He was interviewed by Andrew Edgar (left) and Roger Sayers. Also in the photograph is the Headmaster, Dr Ivan Pollock.

On 8 April 1995 Michael Neill (bugler) and David Russell (piper) played solo in the Last Post ceremony at the Menin Gate in Ypres. This ceremony has taken place every evening at 8 p.m. since 1928, apart from during the Second World War.

Left: Since the introduction of GCSEs, Year 8 pupils have been making an annual visit to Mellifont and Monasterboice monastic sites in the Irish Republic. This photograph shows some of those besieging the Round Tower in Monasterboice in June 1996.

Below: Some Year 9 pupils making a Field Day visit to the Giant's Causeway in 1998. They are accompanied, in the background, by Robin Taylor.

Above: Year 8 pupils, who completed their education at the school in the summer of 2004, visit the Cistercian monastery of Mellifont in Co. Louth in the summer of 1998. Bill Gibson (far right, seated) was to become the most recent Head Prefect.

Right: Paddy Monahan, who teaches French and Spanish, decided to bring a touch of continental authenticity to the school by introducing Boules. As he attempts to direct proceedings in the background, in the summer of 1999, Conal McGready-McKendry demonstrates his versatility by juggling the boules.

Under the direction of Karen Crooks, the Art Department has cultivated some considerable artistic talent amongst the pupils. The College can boast some noted local artists such as Gary Devon and Colin McMaster. Shown here is an oil pastel work, entitled 'My Grandfather', by a recent pupil, John Bell.

On a visit to the battlefields and cemeteries of the Western Front in April 2003, the school party visited Bellewaerde Adventure Park outside Ypres. Richard Bullock (3rd left) took enormous pleasure in frightening the life out of Mark McKee and Chris McIvor (to the left) on the Tower of Death.

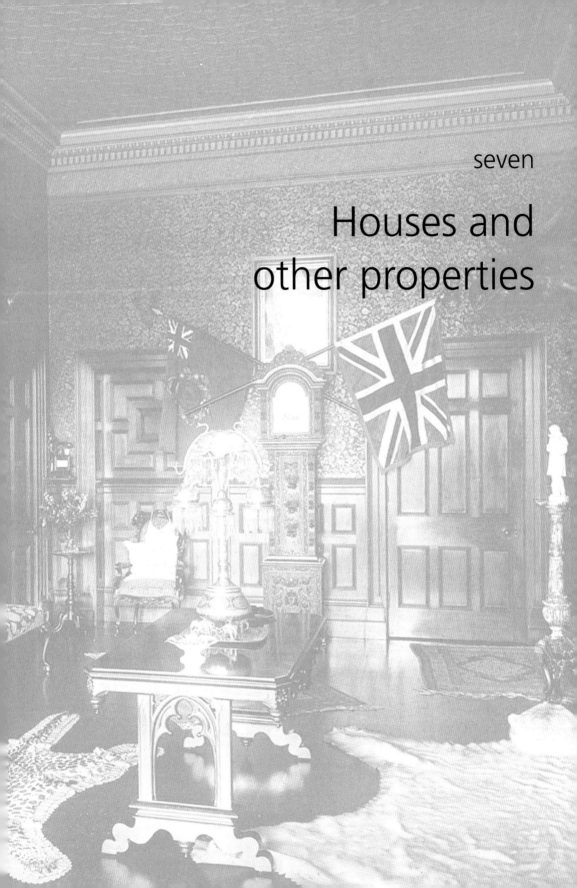

seven

Houses and other properties

During the 1920s, the confidence in Campbell's future was expressed in the expansion of the estate. It absorbed the neighbouring properties of Cabin Hill, Ormiston and Netherleigh – and briefly Tweskard – and effectively doubled the size of the original seventy-acre Belmont estate. These buildings were used as Junior Houses and, in the case of Cabin Hill, as the Prep School.

In 1908, R.A.H. MacFarland imported the concept of the House system to Campbell College, and in that year one Day-boy and four Boarding Houses were created. That number has continued to grow steadily and, until this year, all senior Houses were named after former members of staff.

The original Cabin Hill was constructed by Sam and Martha McTier in 1785. Martha was a sister of Dr William Drennan, United Irishman, who lived there until his death in 1820. The estate was purchased by John Dinnen who built the current house, then bought by the McMordie family in 1902. In 1914 the house was used to store some of the guns from the Larne gun-running. In 1924 it was sold to Campbell as a Junior School, becoming the Prep School in 1929, and finally closing in 2004.

Stanley Sutton, featured with his family and dog, was the Headmaster of Cabin Hill from 1936 to 1967. In this 1938 photograph there are many future professionals, such as schoolteachers, bankers, architects, doctors and legal officials. Future luminaries include Jasper McKee, Professor of Physics and Director of the Cyclotron Laboratory at the University of Manitoba and Sir John MacDermott, Lord Justice of Appeal (son of the later Lord Chief Justice). The address of Vernon Collier was Greenville House, visited in the late eighteenth century by the original occupants of Cabin Hill, Martha McTier and her family!

The young member of staff with the moustache (front row, 6th left) was Francis Cammaerts, who taught at Cabin Hill in the 1937–38 academic year, and ultimately spent fifty years in teaching. He is far more famous as Roger, on whose head the Gestapo placed a high price during the Second World War. Under this pseudonym, Cammaerts ran the Jockey circuit in the south of France, where he became one of the most outstanding secret agents of the War.

Netherleigh was built adjacently to Belmont in 1875 for the Robertson family. In 1921 it was purchased by Samuel Hall-Thompson, who induced the school to buy it in 1928 as a Junior House. It was used during the Second World War as part of the military hospital for officer ranks. The Ministry of Education rented it from the 1940s. As running costs became prohibitive, it was sold to the Department of Finance in the 1970s.

This photograph shows an interior room in Netherleigh, photographed in October 1928, close to the time it was sold to Campbell. Samuel Hall-Thompson later returned to the house when he was appointed Minister of Education in 1944! He sent two of his sons, who were raised in the house, to Campbell College.

Ormiston was built in 1867 in the Scottish Baronial style, and was later occupied by Edward Harland and Lord Pirrie of Harland & Wolff. It was acquired by Campbell College in 1927, providing a school swimming pool. A rifle range was also created in the grounds for the OTC. It became a financial liability and was sold in 1974 and the proceeds used to build a new block bearing the same name in the school grounds.

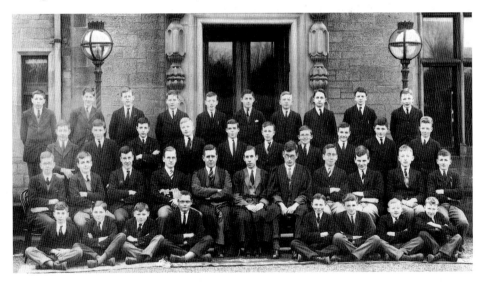

Wilfrid Hutchings – later Headmaster at Armagh Royal School – was the first Housemaster of Ormiston (1927). This photograph, which includes Harris Rundle, who later established an optometrist business, can be dated by the enrolment in January 1928 of two boys sitting front right. The other two members of staff were also recent: OC Kenneth Armour (left of Hutchings), who joined in September 1927, and future Nobel laureate Samuel Beckett, who joined for two terms in January 1928.

Above: Ormiston Junior House photographed in 1973, one year before it was sold. Either side of the dog are the Housemaster, Mr Giles Slaughter – later Headmaster at University College School (Hampstead) – and his wife. His assistants were Michael Caves – later a Housemaster, Head of Mathematics and a Senior Teacher – and Graham Broad, later Headmaster at Rockport Prep School.

The photograph features future Head Prefect (1977-78) Kim Robinson, and Giles Vye, one of three sons of Luther Vye, Headmaster of Cabin Hill. The House Prefect, Andrew Gailey (front, 4th right), later became Housemaster to their Royal Highnesses, Prince William and Harry, at Eton.

Opposite above: The School Prefects with Headmaster John Cook in his final year (1971). They are H.T.M. McMurray, M.A. Vye (son of Luther Vye), W.R.F. Mitchell (son of Bob Mitchell), P.S. Marshall (later on the Cabin Hill staff), B.C. Hanna and J. McCreight; and (front) J.H. Rutherford, R.M. Taylor, M.R. Williams, R.McM. White (Head Prefect), W.B.N. Corry and J.G. Boyd.

Opposite below: In the early 1980s Campbell College briefly accepted Sixth Form girls. Here pictured (1981) with Mrs Doris McGuffin are Elizabeth Ann Loughridge, Angela Scott, Fiona Parker, Tracy Savage, Catherine Dinsmore, Nicole Brand, Caroline Geary, Jane McAlpine, Jane Magowan, Ruth MacNaghten, Kathleen Browne; Alison Watts, Barbara Fair, Kathyrn Smyth, Philippa Holmes, Nicola Smyth, Catherine Lowry, Cherry-Anne Warden, Estelle Munnis, Janet Anderson and Joanne McCausland; Susan Carruthers, Nicola McVeigh, Felicity McCormick, Janice Wilson, Heather Stewart, Leigh Robinson and Janice McClughan.

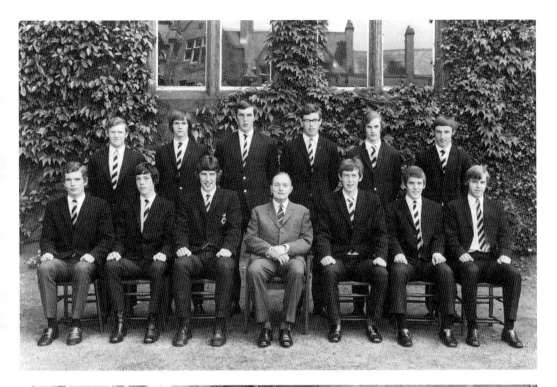

Junior Houses Netherleigh and Ormiston were restored in 1991 when Year 8 pupils (shared with Cabin Hill) were admitted to Campbell, although they were now based in New House.

Netherleigh is photographed here in 1994, with housemaster Ivan Armstrong (centre) – who has since moved to Glenlola Collegiate School – and his assistant, Mark McKee, who is now Housemaster of Price's.

To demonstrate that the rivalry with Ormiston was good-natured, the House Prefect (right of Mr Armstrong) is David Semple, son of Wesley Semple – who was Housemaster of rival Ormiston! David has since established his own coffee business.

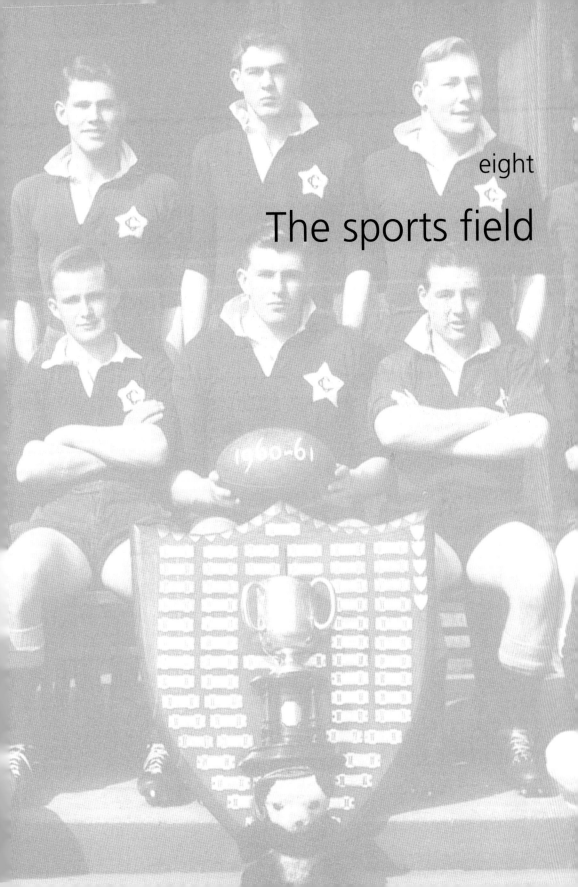

eight

The sports field

Campbell College has, over a century, won every major sporting trophy for which it has competed. The major sports have been available for much of the school's history; others – such as fives, fencing and archery – have been the victims of trends and variable enthusiasm. Campbell has produced success in unexpected sports – such as Irish Grand National winners and champion jockeys.

From 1897 Campbell competed for the most prestigious trophy – the Schools Cup – and has become one of its most successful teams. The College has produced over thirty Irish rugby internationals and, indeed, a double international in the form of Jack Gage (Ireland and South Africa). The school has cultivated many international honours in many sports, competitors and medal-winners in the Commonwealth and Olympic Games, and world record holders (such as Mike Gibson in rugby and David Gotto in squash). The following pages are just a very small sample.

Right: William James Porter lived in Wexford. He played for the 1st XV from 1913 to 1915. He gained a place at Sandhurst. Many, including Headmaster Duff Gibbon, considered that rugby tactics could help to solve military problems. As Intelligence Officer of 2nd Battalion the Leinster Regiment Porter planned one of the War's first daylight raids in January 1917 at Triangle Crater near Loos. He was wounded on 31 July 1917 and died three days later. He is buried at Lijssenthoek Military Cemetery at Poperinghe.

Below: In addition to playing for the 1st XV, William Porter also won an Ulster Schools' representative cap. These caps, along with a number of others, are now in the possession of the school.

Opposite: This photograph shows the 1898-99 1st XV, many of whom had helped to trounce the Ulster XV in December 1897 by 36-0, and had won the Schools Cup for the first occasion in 1898. Coached by Henry Hirsch, the team included Barnett (Barry) Allison, who was selected to play for the senior Irish international team in 1899 whilst still at school.

The 1922 Schools Cup-winning team, coached by Raywood Beaven, comprised Kirk Forsythe (later the school doctor), F.P.K. Breakey, G.L. Millington, D.McM. Carson and V.C.G.M. Gibson; seated: W.S. Roome (later a Chief of Police in Ontario), H.I. McClure, J.H. McElney, M.V. Delap (captain), R.M. Byers, P.H. Perry, and (sitting) H.W. Bailie, G.P. McCullagh, H.C.M. Stone and A.R. Ewart. In 1924, Stone was given a small replica cup for having won three consecutive finals.

1st XV practice takes place on Longfield. One of the players appears to be John Harold McElney, captain of the Schools Cup-winning team of 1923, which suggests that this photograph was taken around this time. McElney lost one brother in each World War.

The 1953-1954 Cabin Hill XV features two future Irish rugby internationals and British Lions – Ken Kennedy (seated, 2nd left) and Mike Gibson (sitting, left). Also in the team are Mike Gibson's brother, Peter, later a judge; Derry Whyte, now Hon secretary of the OC Society; David Thompson, who became Headmaster of Harding Memorial School in East Belfast; and John Park, a Consultant Obstetrician and Gynaecologist.

Mike Gibson played a record 69 times for Ireland between 1964 and 1979, and gained another twelve caps on five British Lions' tours, 1966-1977. Ken Kennedy also appeared for the Lions between 1966 and 1974, and 45 times as Irish hooker from 1965 to 1975. Here they are pictured (two main figures on the left) playing for the Lions against Poverty Bay in New Zealand.

Cecil Pedlow earned thirty caps for Ireland between 1952 and 1962. He was selected for the Barbarians team in the late 1950s, and is here seen scoring the second try of their opening match on the Lions' 1955 tour to South Africa. He is a double Irish international, having played squash for Ireland, and in 1952 he was the Irish Junior Tennis champion.

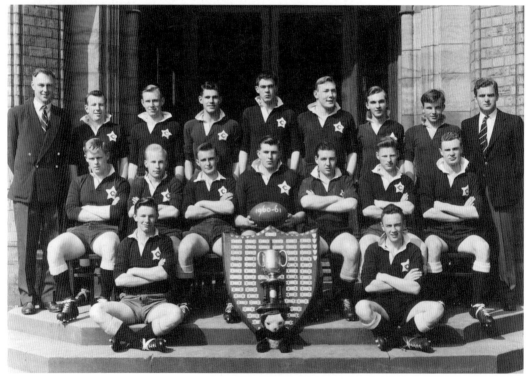

Under the coaching of Bob Mitchell and David Young, Campbell enjoyed sixteen Schools Cup final appearances in twenty years to 1970. One of those victorious teams was that of 1961. Captained by Freddie Craig, it contained six Interprovincial players, including Mike Gibson, the most-capped Irish international rugby player.

Campbell has produced many Interprovincial rugby players, but 1964 proved an exceptional year with five: Roger Stephens, Derek Spence, Mansell Heslip (also captain), Kelly Wilson and Ron Fox.

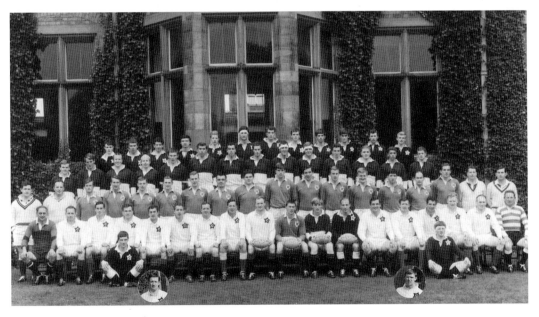

On 1 October 1966, a crowd of over 4,000 turned out to watch two matches – which boasted over twenty internationals – held to inaugurate Fox's Field as the new home of the 1st XV. The 1st XV played an OC XV, and a Mike Gibson's XV challenged the Combined Universities of Ireland.

Walter Jones, the team captain, receives the Schools Cup at Ravenhill, March 1968. Also looking on are M.G. Allingham, G.A. Blair and I.C.L. Gleadhill. Walter is now Headmaster of Royal Grammar School Worcester, and the other three are based in Wales, Scotland and Northern Ireland!

The Campbell tour party visited British Columbia, Easter 1972. The group comprises eight future solicitors, two doctors, a North Sea oil driller, a vet and a jeweller. Jeremy Taylor is vice-principal at Fleming Fulton school; Mark Lambert is an actor and theatre director; Guy Beringer became Senior Partner in a London legal firm; and Michael Quee is Head Groundsman at Campbell. Tim Martin bought his first pub in 1979, and now runs the ever-expanding J.D. Wetherspoon empire.

With two minutes left against Australia in the 1991 World Cup, OC Gordon Hamilton made a 40 yard dash to the line; his try seemed destined to take Ireland into a semi-final against New Zealand – but sadly, the Australians had time to respond to leave the Irish disappointed.

Brian Robinson, now Head of PE at Campbell, scores one of his record-equalling four tries in a match against Zimbabwe in the 1991 World Cup.

Above: Neil McComb and the 1st XV squad celebrate victory at Ravenhill in March 2002. Neil was selected for the Ulster Schools' XV, and the Irish Under-19 and Under-21 squads.

Below: The old pavilion was incorporated into an extended version, officially opened in October 1932 in memory of the OC Irish rugby international, William Fraser Browne. It is pictured here in 1996 in 'A' Level artwork by Shaun Wilson, which features 1st XI cricketer, Rory Wallace.

The first cricket XI of 1895-1896 comprised: R.M. Gage, T.B. Shaw (umpire), J.H. Moore, F.W. Crofts (scorer), Mr Lovett (professional), R.B. Dunwoody, R. Gething and C.D. Fisher; seated are J.A. Shillidy, E.L. MacNaughten, B. Gething, G.R. Thompson (captain), J.B. Allison, H.S. McClelland and J.S. Rogers. Barry Allison was also an Irish rugby international; George Thompson returned as a teacher in 1900; and Freeman Wills Crofts became a noted writer of detective fiction.

The captain of the 1937 1st XI was Stuart Pollock who was to represent Ireland at cricket and squash, and was an Interprovincial player in four sports! Seated is J.T. Shepherd who developed an international medical reputation. T.T. Fulton and G.W. Houston are also notable in the medical profession. Geoffrey Alderdice (front left) won the DFC in the Second World War, as did (seated, left) the future Air Marshal Sir Alfred Ball – plus the DSO and US Air Medal.

Left: Hockey only began as a regular sport in 1934. Coaching was led by OC Kenneth Armour, and a number of individuals attained representative status including, in 1950, Oliver Eaton and Robin Bailey. Robin (right) won seventeen caps for Ireland, and became the captain of the international squad (1958-1960). Oliver, who captained the Interprovincial team in 1951, was murdered by the IRA in July 1976.

Below: Kenneth Armour (left) and Edward Agnew coached the 1st XI to its first victory in the Burney Cup in 1957. The team was N.McB. McAlpin, J.A.F. Burns, P.H.H McMeekin, B.M. Adams, J.G. Wolseley and V.C. Haslett; and (front) D.A. Johnston, D.C. Kernohan, A.L. Hailes (captain), B.B. Bolton and R.M. Brown. Alan Hailes became a producer and director at Ulster TV. Victor Haslett became a Chairman of the Sports Council of NI; and James Burns is an older brother of *The Krypton Factor*'s Gordon.

The only other Burney Cup victory was in 1986, when the team was Andrew Rebbeck, Hector Taylor, David Miller, Simon Gordon, Roger Lowry, Nicholas Thompson, and (seated) Mark Rebbeck, William Jack, Peter Priestley (captain), Richard Owens, Alan Corry and Andrew McMillan. Ted Cooke (left) was the coach.

The Hockey 1st XI reached the Burney Cup final again in 1999, the same year in which the 2nd XI, pictured here at Blaris under captain Tristan Barry, reached the Dowdall final. Pictured with the team is coach Russell Birch, who retired in the same year, after twenty-five years at Campbell. He started on the staff in 1962, and some of his career was spent at Belfast Royal Academy.

The 1939 Athletics squad is seen here under the captaincy of Desmond Houston, who was soon to win the Military Cross in Burma. To the left is Basil Tweedie who, in 1940, in addition to several other victories, set a shot putt record of 45 ft 8 ins (13.93m) which has still never been beaten! Charles Nodder (front right), as a prisoner-of-war, was renowned for making secret radio sets out of a variety of scrap.

On 30 January 1957, at the Northern Ireland Schools Cross Country Championship, the first six team members home ensured victory. Presented with the cup were: A.J. Wilson, S.E.B Acheson, J.G. Neill, N.I.A. Irwin, N. L. Taggart and D.A. McDonald.

Above: Over the decades there have been many outstanding athletes at the school. However, the athletics facilities left something to be desired until, through the vision of Headmaster Brian Wilson, an all-weather surface – which doubles as three hockey pitches during the winter months – was opened in 1982.

Right: Russell Birch was always in charge of the High Jump on Sports Day. Here in the summer of 1999, clearly absorbed by another event, are Paul Budden, Andrew McCord and (partially hidden) Samuel Poots.

Above: In 1933 half of those in the Imperial Cadet shooting tour to Canada came from Campbell College. Amongst those at the back are Peter Warnock, who died only five years later, Ian Macaulay, H.W.C. Bailie and J.S. Fetherston, one of five brothers at the school. With Commanding Officer Charles Bowen of the staff at the front are J.A. Smith, J.H.F. MacGiffin, later a team manager at the Commonwealth Games, and F.R. Ievers, who (like Macaulay) died in the Second World War.

Right: Leaving Campbell in 1969, David Calvert became an RAF pilot, flying Vulcan bombers and Phantom fighters from 1975 to 1991. He has been a flying instructor since 1996, but is probably best known on the international Target Rifle Shooting circuit. In 2002 he helped Ireland to win the National Challenge Trophy. He has won four gold and three bronze medals in seven Commonwealth Games appearances for Northern Ireland, and has aspirations to compete in ten such competitions.

Above: Andrew Bree is one of Ireland's leading swimmers, and since 1998 has participated in Commonwealth, European and World Championships. He is pictured here in action in the European Swimming Short Course Championships in Dublin on 11 December 2003 in the 100m breaststroke contest. Three days later he won the silver medal in the 200m breaststroke final in 2 minutes 2.08 seconds. During the meeting he broke five Irish records.

Left: The Hoey family has produced several remarkable golfers who have played at representative level. Michael Hoey – who was Ulster Schools Champion in 1996, Irish Boys' Champion in 1997 and Irish Open Amateur Champion in 1998 – was selected for the 2001 Walker Cup, and turned professional in April 2002. Michael is shown with the 2001 British Amateur Matchplay Championship trophy.

Boxing emerged as a more popular sporting pastime with the arrival of Gibbon in the 1920s. Some of the fighting weights included paper, gnat and mosquito! The 1925-26 squad comprised R.B. Rainsford, D.W. Baird, F.A.L. Harrison, J.McA. Irons, W.B. Macready, C.P. Magill, E.F. Parker, C.W.E.N.C. Pelly, C.C. McCreight, C.C. Ewart, F.R. Ievers, and (at the front) W.C Stewart and H.L.C. Fraser.

Archery arrived at Campbell in the late 1970s. Peter Lawson became a member of a Commonwealth Games team, and John Keers was an Irish Under-18 champion archer.

Opposite above: Coached by David Young, the 1968 tennis team included I.S. Bennett, L.M. McClure, D.C. Hill, and (front) N.J.R. Mullan, M.R. Whitlock (captain), A.D.L. Green and J.R. McKelvey.

Opposite below: In this 1950 Cabin Hill soccer photograph are I.H. Watson, R.D. Galway, J.M. Miller, M.J.M. Gooding, W.D.L. Pollock and T.D. Singleton. Seated are G.K. Siggins, D.W. Harkness, J.C.M. Lynn (captain), B.D.E. Marshall (later Irish rugby international) and H.C. McCall (Irish cricket international). David Harkness became Professor of Irish History at QUB, and T.D. Singleton coached the 1998 Bermuda Olympic Luge team! The staff are Headmaster Stanley Sutton and Thomas 'Titch' McMurray.

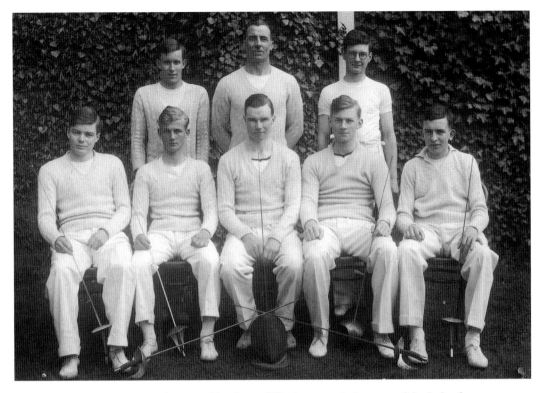

Fencing has fluctuated in popularity, and has been difficult to sustain because of the lack of competition. The first inter-school match in Ireland took place against Blackrock College on 19 November 1938. Pictured is the 1939 team, coached by Instructor R.S.M. Miller, which includes Basil Tweedie.

Volleyball has become more popular in recent years. The 2002 team comprised James Taylor, Ben Toland, Adam Campbell, and (front) Paul Sweeney, Tom Napier, Ryan Whiteside and Piers Browning. Tom and Adam were picked for the Northern Ireland Under-19 squad.

Above: A staff versus pupil soccer match was played in the summer of 1995; the staff team included Phil Dermott, Robin Gordon, Paddy Monahan, Alan Cluff, Cameron Hunter, John McKinney, Terry Koch (ex-Linfield FC), Mark McKee and John Knox. Rear left is Head Prefect Chris Gibson.

Right: In addition to being in the school Shooting, Fencing and Boxing teams, Basil Tweedie (right) was a member of the 2nd XI Hockey team, captain of Athletics, captain of the school and Ulster cricket teams, and a member of the school and Ulster Rugby XV. George Jackson was Head Prefect and CSM of the JTC. He was also captain of Rugby and Hockey, and played 1st XI cricket. He represented Ulster at all three games. They both left Campbell in 1940, and within three years they were victims of the Second World War. *Ne Obliviscaris.*

Other local titles published by Tempus

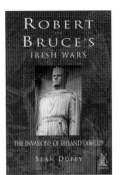

Robert the Bruce's Irish Wars
The Invasion of Ireland 1306–1329
SEÁN DUFFY

Much is known about Robert the Bruce's military campaigns for Scottish Independence in Scotland and England but what about his expeditions to Ireland? In 1315 a fleet-load of Bannockburn veterans put ashore on the coast of modern-day County Antrim. It was a major undertaking and this lavishly illustrated study tells the story of the invasion itself and the battles that followed.
0 7524 1974 9

A History of the Black Death in Ireland
MARIA KELLY

Transported by rats and fleas in the trading vessels plying between Ireland, England and France, the plague appeared in Dublin and Drogheda in the summer of 1348. It spread quickly and virulently, reaching south towards Waterford, Youghal, Cork and Limerick and wiping out whole communities in its path. Maria Kelly goes in search of the 'Great Pestilence' whose consequences are often obscured by the intricate and tumultuous history of the time, and traces how the Irish reacted to this seemingly invisible killer.
0 7524 3185 4

Irish Sea Shipping Publicised
R.N. FORSYTHE

The companies that operated across the Irish Sea have been using posters, pamphlets, brochures and guides for over two hundred years in an effort to attract custom, whether passenger or freight. This book considers Irish Sea trade from Swansea in Wales to Campbeltown in the west of Scotland and from Cork to Londonderry, using original guide books, posters and pamphlets and photographs.
0 7524 2355 X

Ireland's Round Towers
TADHG O'KEEFFE

The round tower is Ireland's most distinctive medieval monument. This book explores the towers' qualities as works of architecture as well as examining their relationships with other buildings at the sites on which they stand. The author argues that the towers were employed in ceremonies and other ritualised activities of the Church in Ireland. They should be seen as crucial evidence in a new history of Irish Christianity between the Viking raids and the late twelfth-century Norman invasion.
0 7524 2571 4

If you are interested in purchasing other books published by Tempus, or in case you have difficulty finding any Tempus books in your local bookshop, you can also place orders directly through our website

www.tempus-publishing.com